Praise for J. Tucker Miller and

The First Four Words

Over the years I've watched as professionals at all levels struggle to have hard conversations. Most avoid conflict out of fear that the conversation will backfire or destroy an important relationship. *The First Four Words* inspires readers to move beyond avoidance to curiosity, and from curiosity to possibility. I sincerely believe this book will help more people have these necessary conversations, with positive outcomes.

– Mikaela Kiner

Founder and CEO of Reverb
and Author, Female Firebrands

The First Four Words offers a game-changing strategy for those of us who are uncertain about starting difficult conversations. Author and executive coach Tucker Miller has cracked the code by illustrating how four words can foster understanding and collaboration.

– Michelle Marchant

Senior Employment Attorney,
Formerly with Hewlett Packard and Microsoft

Tucker Miller's extraordinary new book, *The First Four Words,* gives us simple, usable tools to make sure even our most challenging talks strike the right tone beginning with our very first few words. Why's this important: because many important conversations never take place or start off wrong and never recover. Why: because we just don't know what to say. This happens at work, with family, and in other day-to-day situations. Tucker's distilled a lifetime of personal and professional wisdom to give us a vital, practical guide for launching meaningful conversations where understanding and impact are so critical.

– Stephen M. Paskoff

Founder, President & CEO
Employment Learning Innovations, Inc.

When Tucker Miller told me about her new book, I ordered ten copies! As an executive coach myself, *The First Four Words* is a book I plan to give to every one of my clients. *The First Four Words* is just what I've needed to share with leaders I support. In her book, Tucker Miller brings her usual wisdom, insight and empathy to this important topic in a way that will help all of us in business and in life!

– Kristina Moris

Founder and President of The Washington Firm, Ltd.

Tucker Miller puts a new spin on how leaders can more easily engage people into meaningful conversations. As she explains in her book, *The First Four Words*, "Eliminating the tendency to avoid difficult conversations is key to honing leadership capabilities and preparing for expanded roles of influence and impact. Your success comes from showing up and sharing your opinion, and your ability to do that lies just on the other side of avoiding discomfort." Throughout my career I have witnessed leaders avoid the difficult conversations because they are not comfortable in having them. Her practical strategy will help leaders communicate more confidently and effectively.

– Marilyn Thiet

Certified Business Coach, President and CEO of EDGE Performance Acceleration

I am thrilled to endorse Tucker Miller and her book, *The First Four Words*. *The First Four Words* is not just a book; it's a roadmap for those who understand that the key to success lies in the subtle nuances of conversation. I wholeheartedly recommend this book to anyone eager to elevate their communication game and make a lasting impact both professionally and personally. Prepare to be inspired, enlightened, and equipped with the tools to unlock the true potential of your words.

– Bruce M Pflaumer

Founder of Michael Bruce Image Consulting and host of The Wisdom of the Wardrobe *podcast*

As much as I appreciate models and tools for how to have a meaningful conversation, in the heat of the moment I can't recall any of it. *The First Four Words* eliminates that problem by providing a strategy that's easy to remember, apply and practice. Drawing on her experience as a business leader and executive coach, Tucker Miller has provided an invaluable resource that inspires and instructs.

– Alison Talbot

Senior Human Resources Executive
for national insurance company

So many leaders, from the CEO on down, struggle with knowing what to say to start an important conversation. As a result, they avoid the conversations they should be having to strengthen relationships, build trust and resolve conflicts. *The First Four Words* is just the resource I've needed to support and inspire my clients to reach out and engage. It's not a gimmick – it's a practical and easy to remember tool that can help anyone seeking a method to communicate more clearly and effectively. I look forward to sharing it with my team and all the leaders I support. Highly recommend!

– Marie Tjernlund

President and Executive Coach, Noble Edge Consulting

the first four words

the first four words

a fresh approach to starting conversations with ease and confidence

j. tucker miller

Advantage | Books

Published by Advantage Books, Charleston, South Carolina.
An imprint of Advantage Media.

ADVANTAGE is a registered trademark, and the Advantage colophon is a trademark of Advantage Media Group, Inc.

Printed in the United States of America.

10 9 8 7 6 5 4 3 2 1

ISBN: 978-1-64225-977-3 (Paperback)
ISBN: 978-1-64225-976-6 (eBook)

Library of Congress Control Number: 2024905345

Cover design by David Taylor.
Layout design by Matthew Morse.

Advantage Books is an imprint of Advantage Media Group. Advantage Media helps busy entrepreneurs, CEOs, and leaders write and publish a book to grow their business and become the authority in their field. Advantage authors comprise an exclusive community of industry professionals, idea-makers, and thought leaders. For more information go to **advantagemedia.com**.

To Matthew and Meredith,
who came into the world as my children
and have become my friends and guides.

And to Wilma,
whose enthusiasm for her daughter writing a book
has been a tremendous source of joy for both of us.

contents

about the author

J. Tucker Miller is an author, executive coach, and master facilitator. She's also a lawyer, but don't hold that against her.

With over thirty-five years of business and senior leadership experience in the fields of law, human resources, sales, and consulting, Ms. Miller is a sought-after speaker who has delivered training and workshops to thousands of participants. She is passionate about inspiring leaders to engage more purposefully with authenticity, courage, and humanity.

A former Air Force brat who moved around a lot when she was growing up, Tucker is happy to call the Pacific Northwest home. She and her husband have been married over thirty years. Ms. Miller is available for speaking events and invites you to connect with her at her website, www.JTuckerMiller.com.

introduction

Have you ever felt you needed to say something to someone but then convinced yourself not to do it? Perhaps you imagined it would be too hard or it might not go well. You may have feared that the other person would react badly. You may have even convinced yourself you didn't know what to say.

Somewhere between thinking you should have a conversation and imagining how it might go, you decided to neglect it altogether and hoped things would resolve themselves on their own. But here's the problem: they rarely do. More often than not, issues tend to fester over time and, as they do, they become harder to solve.

If you can relate to any of this, this book is for you. If you want to make it easier to engage in conversations—especially those that are difficult, unfamiliar, or uncomfortable—this book is for you. If you are a leader of a team, this book is for you. If you have been agonizing about how to **start** conversations, or if you've been uncomfortable asking for what you want or providing feedback, this book is for you.

Who Should Read This Book

You deserve to be heard. Your opinions matter. While I have written this book with business leaders in mind, the concepts can be applied to initiate conversations with teams, colleagues, friends, and family members, helping you engage in conversations that matter in work and in life.

Why I Wrote This Book

I'm on a mission to convince you that starting a conversation is a lot easier than you might imagine. I also know that once you **start** a conversation, more often than not, you'll finish the conversation. It may not be perfect, it may not be smooth—but once started, you're more than halfway through. It's walking away that undermines results, relationships, and confidence.

So, what if beginning these conversations could be so simple that there would be no reason *not* to have them? Throughout this book, I will demonstrate that you don't need scripts or complex conversational models to be successful in engaging someone in conversation. To the contrary, with only a few words to get started, you can achieve deeper understanding, engagement, and connection.

Overcoming Resistance

The number one reason why conversations fail is simply because they don't happen. Fear, uncertainty, and discomfort are a few of the reasons why people avoid asking for what they truly want and need. The stories we tell ourselves before even starting a conversation are the biggest barriers to achieving what we want. These narratives are rarely based on fact. As I coach clients, I often answer their resistance to, for example, giving feedback to a team member, by asking, "Is that really true they will react that way?" and "How do you know it's true?" Often, the reason for not giving feedback has little to do with reality and is based, instead, on story and justification. Avoiding conversations actually makes things worse: frustration mounts, poor performance is protracted, resentment and distrust increase.

This is the dilemma I've felt as a leader from time to time, whether considering conversations with team members or persons to whom I've reported. And it's a challenge I see frequently with my clients. How do you overcome natural inclinations to play it safe and avoid conflict when circumstances require boldness and honesty? My quest to solve this conundrum is what led to this book.

From Resistance to Possibility

Inspiration is the birth-child of being in nature. On one of my frequent hikes through my Pacific Northwest neighborhood trails, while pondering how to help people more confidently converse with one another, I recalled the classic game show I watched when I was young, *Name That Tune.* A segment of that show involved contestants facing off with each other and declaring that they could "name that tune" in only a few musical notes. They would go back and forth, daring each other to name the tune in eight, five, or four notes, sometimes even fewer. If the person who bid the lowest was successful, they were the winner.

Well begun is half done.

—MARY POPPINS

Once a conversation is started, half the work is done, but on my mission to fine-tune these exchanges, I wondered if there was a sweet spot for how many words were effective in starting a conversation. If people were open to the **possibility** that having a conversation was as simple as starting it with just a few words, they might move away from excuses and rationalizing their lack of action and instead engage in meaningful conversations. Finding those opening words might even feel more like a game. Once they became open to the idea that there was an easy and effective way to **start** the conversation, might leaders find themselves having more timely, proactive, and meaningful conversations? The answer turned out to be *yes*, and the number of words was surprisingly few.

Just Four Words

As I worked with clients, I consistently observed that as few as four words, adapted to the particular circumstance, were all it took to **start** a conversation. You might question, then, if only four, why not one, or two, or three? I had the same thought. My observations, experimentation, and interviews have convinced me, however, that fewer words consistently fall short. One or two words can feel peremptory, demanding, even rude. Anna, a colleague, also explained that her one-word responses often conveyed to her husband that she was distracted or uninterested.

So, while one or two words were often too few, it became clear that ten words were too many. The more words, the less **clarity**. Ultimately, I came to see four words as a sweet spot—memorable, succinct, and straightforward. Starting a conversation might be as simple as any of these:

- *"Let's have a conversation."*
- *"When are you free?"*
- *"I'd like your opinion."*
- *"Please help me understand."*

Sounds simple, right? And it is. Time and time again, I've seen that once the conversation is started, the conversation is had.

Whole conversations could be built around simple four-word phrases to **start**, additional four-word phrases to keep the conversation going, and a few four-word phrases to conclude a conversation that amounted to meaningful, memorable, and strategically transformational conversations. I observed that not only did this work well, just as in the *Name That Tune* game show, this strategy actually resulted in people feeling more empowered. This simple approach was fresh and, dare I say it, even fun. The question of what to say became far less daunting and invoked puzzle-solving **curiosity**, and I discovered people more readily leaning into conversations instead of avoiding them.

Better Communication Is Fundamental to Good Leadership

While the focus of this book is on ways to **start** a conversation, this is first and foremost a book on leadership. Think of me as your advisor and your coach as you read the following pages. I want to help you engage people more effectively with greater ease and confidence. Eliminating the tendency to avoid difficult conversations is key to honing leadership capabilities and preparing for expanded roles of influence and impact. Your success comes from showing up and sharing your opinion, and your ability to do that lies just on the other side of avoiding discomfort.

Ultimately, while I sincerely hope this book instills a new sense of **possibility** and encouragement for how to have conversations you may have previously avoided, I also hope you find this approach to be fresh, simple, and practical, and that it produces more of the results you want. Choosing four words—the words that will initially engage your listening—is both strategic and kind. You're breaking things down so that you can be heard and your listener can hear the invitation to the conversation.

Allow me to offer some useful tips:

- First and foremost, have fun with this approach. Whether you view this as a game or a puzzle, the process of condensing a message into four words engages your brain creatively, moving you from fear to **curiosity**, from curiosity to **possibility**.
- Always bear in mind the bigger goals: collaboration, understanding, and **clarity**.
- Develop a few four-word phrases to invite conversation. There is no way to write a script for every meaningful conversation, but you can plan where your conversation might go.
- Avoid phrases with fewer than four words. (I'll explain why in the next chapter.)
- Keep it **simple**: contractions are allowed; hyphenated words count as one word.
- Don't get so stuck on the rules that you sacrifice meaning. If it turns out to be five or six words, that's OK, but challenge yourself to think of a four-word phrase. (This will also be explained in the next chapter.)
- And finally, be mindful of phrases that will likely do more harm than good. For instance, I've yet to find a situation

where starting a conversation with "over my dead body" works well. (I'll share more examples in chapter ten.)

What You Will Find in This Book

As I take you on a journey through different conversational scenarios, I want to show you that starting a difficult conversation is easier than you may think. I'll share some stories and examples and suggest some four-word phrases for you to use. I have intentionally created space for you to jot down some four-word phrases of your own, and I invite you to try some of the exercises and reflections provided at the end of each chapter.

- Chapter one will provide information about why starting a conversation with four words works so well and how this strategy helps to overcome our natural tendency to avoid challenging conversations.
- Chapter two is for leaders, in particular. I will identify the most important conversations leaders have with their team members, and I will provide some examples of how to address these critical areas and why they should not be avoided or postponed.
- Chapter three focuses on building and maintaining trust. We'll look at real-world examples of trust gone wrong, and I'll provide examples of how to get better at building and maintaining trust.
- Chapter four provides strategies for building consensus and navigating through conflict at work or in life.
- Chapter five offers examples and inspiration for encouraging each other at home and at work.

- Chapter six is definitely for everyone. It is about networking and how to overcome resistance when it comes to attending events. I'll also offer some tips on how you can break the ice to build connections. The goal for this chapter is to get you thinking about how to build your social and professional network and to find fun in doing it.
- Chapter seven is to assure you that the concepts and skills introduced in this book are not just for work. In this chapter we'll look at real-life examples and strategies for smoothing family gatherings. This will give you a chance to practice the concepts described in this book with people you love and presumably will continue to love even if things don't go as well as you hope.
- Chapter eight is about hard times. What do you say to each other in the middle of a setback or grief? I was struck while writing this chapter about how much tragedy I've witnessed in my life and in the lives of those I care about. This chapter will help you show up more fully for someone in need of comfort.
- Chapter nine is about deepening understanding and building connections. This is certainly a theme throughout this book, and this chapter offers some examples of ways to move beyond starting a conversation and building stronger ties with others in your life.
- Chapter ten will help you avoid applying our "four word" strategy in ways that will likely make things worse. Consider, for example, "over my dead body." In the moment, such a quip might seem funny or clever, but such a dismissive comment may cause lasting damage to the relationship.
- Chapter eleven explores what to do if "four words" just isn't working. I share other ideas and permission to try alternatives.

- Chapter twelve answers, at least in part, what's next. What do you do after starting a conversation? Where do you go from here? Spoiler alert: I suggest keeping the conversation going by being vulnerable with others. Being vulnerable doesn't just happen, but opening up to each other becomes easier over time as a result of the investment of conversation, deeper understanding, and reconciliation when tensions flare.

How to Use This Book

As you explore the contents, feel free to jump around. You'll see that I offer examples for a variety of settings and situations, as well as some suggested activities and experiments that you can do on your own or with teams (and family members). Let this book be a source of insight and inspiration; let it also be your journal. I want you to **experiment**, play, and assess as you go along. I've made reference to research and relevant analytics for those requiring data and proof that this four-word strategy actually works. (My editor suggested that would be important to some of you.) To that, I say: *You are very welcome.*

Bear in mind that the value of this book is best realized when put into action. To add opportunities for both insight and practice, you'll find some exercises and challenges at the end of each chapter. I encourage you to make notes along the way and invent your own four-word phrases to experiment with and add to your toolbox.

So, buckle up. It's about to get fun.

Try This

As I experimented with four-word phrases to start conversations, I engaged my family in some of the fun. With my two college-age children having returned home to wait out the early months of the pandemic, I shared my four-word ideas with my family of four (no pun intended). We immediately started brainstorming. I laid out a big sheet of white poster paper on our dining room table, and as we came up with phrases, we would jot them down. This activity in itself prompted even more conversation as we reacted to each other's ideas and tested things out during dinner. We quickly discovered that, to be effective, a promising four-word opening requires a sincere, engaging delivery. The tone of delivery significantly impacted whether the outcome of starting the conversation would end in success or failure.

As I shared my ideas with friends, many of them started keeping track on their fingers how many words they were using. I would notice their hands moving, and then see them smile. "You're right, it was just four," they'd say.

I answered, "Not always, but often."

With your team or your family, explain the premise of four-word phrases that could initiate a conversation, or which might be useful in the context of an interaction. Place a poster-sized sheet of paper on a wall or table, have some markers available, and invite people to brainstorm and add examples. Note: you may need to set some ground rules about inappropriate words or comments to ensure that the exercise remains productive and fun for everyone. In addition to brainstorming phrases, consider testing them out with different tones of voice or in different situations. Discuss what works well and why. You may also identify phrases that you prefer not be used with each other.

My Four Words

My Four Words

one

the power of four

Four Words at a Glance

- *I won the lottery!*
- *I just got promoted.*
- *We're moving to Australia.*
- *Will you marry me?*
- *We're having a baby.*

Each of these statements has the power to change the trajectory of a person's life in some capacity. Notice that it doesn't take much to get someone's attention. Think about news headlines. Short phrases are enough to draw people in, creating pause and igniting **curiosity**. Our attention is interrupted, and suddenly we are determined to find out the rest of the story. Like those leading headlines, in as few as four words, you can start an impactful conversation. Bottom line: **Start** strong; don't bury the lede!

Engage Listening with a Few Words

Regardless of what your story is about, it's up to the leader to obtain interest from the audience. Look around as you talk. Are people distracted? Are they scrolling through their phones? Are they nodding off? The barometer for how engaging you are is right in front of you. Blaming millennials, short attention spans, COVID-19, too many online meetings, and the like will explain only part of why you're losing them. At the end of the day, leaders have a responsibility to communicate in ways that will attract the attention of their colleagues. If people aren't listening, try changing things up.

Brevity Enhances Clarity; Clarity Engages Attention

Have you ever asked someone to take a look at something, and their first question has to do with how long the task will take? Rather than asking what it is you want from them, they are more focused on how much of their time you plan on taking up.

Certainly, attention spans aren't what they used to be. Studies have shown that in the last ten years, attention spans have shortened dramatically. Where the average length of a commercial was sixty seconds a decade ago, today's ads can be as short as ten or fifteen seconds.[1] Why the

1 "Ad Length Impact on Attention Is Minimal—but Content Tips the Scales | Research Mountain," MNTN Research, accessed February 9, 2024, https://research.mountain.com/creative-analysis/ad-length-impact-on-attention-is-minimal-but-content-tips-the-scales/.; MediaRadar, "Are Traditional TV Ads Really Getting Shorter? [Updated 2019 Numbers]," last modified January 10, 2019, https://mediaradar.com/blog/are-traditional-tv-ads-really-getting-shorter-2019-numbers/.; "TV Commercial Length for Effective Advertising," Go Localise (blog), April 14, 2022, https://golocalise.com/blog/tv-commercial-length-for-effective-advertising.

change? People begin to tune out, scroll, or swipe if they're exposed to longer ads.

As a leader, you can capture and hold the attention of even the most distractible listener in one of two ways: tell a story or keep your message brief and impactful. Our brains love stories.[2] Seen a TED Talk lately? Stories cut through distractions and pull listeners into the action, causing them to anticipate what will happen next, and invest in the characters and outcome. Stories connect us through shared experiences and are great ways to illustrate key points.

Regardless of whether storytelling is in your personal wheelhouse, everyone has the ability for **brevity**. Notice, though, how rarely you experience **brevity** in the meetings you attend. How many times do presentations begin with apologies or elaborate business cases to introduce the message? Too often people begin with the rationale instead of the point. Worse, by the time you get to the point you want to make, you may have lost your audience. Ironically, the more words you use to make your point, the less you communicate.

- Wordiness dilutes the message.
- Wordiness creates unnecessary confusion.
- If you're using too many words, you're likely saying nothing.

Let Brevity Be Your Differentiator

Save the business case, the research, the data and analytics, and get to the point. Don't get me wrong ... the details are important; have them available to respond to questions and objections *after* you've captured the attention of your audience.

---

2 American Psychological Association, "Speaking of Psychology: The Ever-Shortening Human Attention Span," Podcast audio, May 16, 2022, https://www.apa.org/news/podcasts/speaking-of-psychology/attention-spans.

With fewer words, carefully chosen to capture attention, you stand a better chance of being heard. Fewer words also allow you to slow down. When people have limited time to make their point, rather than strategically planning what they intend to convey, they often talk faster. Faster is not clearer. Worse, it may sound like static to the listener.

Whenever you are speaking, whether it's to a group or one on one, consider it your moment for influence and leadership. You lead by making yourself heard and understood, and believe it or not, you can have more impact with fewer words. Make up your mind, take a stand, express an opinion. And if circumstances allow for more time, *then* invite discussion and questions. People inevitably listen best when they feel that their opinions matter too.

A Story About Too Many Words

Why do people overexplain and use too many words when a mere few would do? In some instances, they may be looking for reassurance or acknowledgment. In other situations, they might offer unsolicited details to be helpful where none was sought. (Have you ever complimented Aunt Jackie on her Jell-O salad and found yourself getting the play-by-play instructions for how to make it when you actually hope to never have it again?)

In general, speakers overexplain either because they didn't take the time to sharpen their message, or because they want to soften a message they fear will provoke a negative response. Prioritizing being nice over being clear results in unnecessary frustrations and breakdowns. Allow me to contribute a personal example, one which my husband, Warner, authorized me to share. Warner and I repeated some version of the following conversation over a period of four weeks.

He asked if I wanted a home treadmill.

"No, I don't want a treadmill in our house," I said. I had several reasons for my response and, without taking breath, I proceeded to list them all. "I think a treadmill is too big; it takes up too much room; it's too heavy; we don't have enough ceiling height; it will be too noisy; I don't want to give up our family room or guest room to accommodate it; I don't understand why we don't make more effort to go to the Y or get outside. Besides, if you like biking, wouldn't you rather have a stationary bike? Why not get a bike since our son works for a bike company?"

I thought that would be the end of it, but at least three more times over the ensuing weeks Warner lovingly turned to me and said, "Hon, do you think we should get a treadmill? Is that something you would like? Do you think you would use it?"

I'll leave my exasperated response to your imagination, largely because the truth of it doesn't put me in a good light. Every time the question of a treadmill came up, I would answer as I had before with even more reasons for why I didn't want one.

These conversations with Warner left me bewildered and frustrated. Was he not listening? Or was it possible that he really wanted a treadmill and wasn't saying it? Was he trying to convince me by asking me repeatedly?

Our final round on this topic led me to throw my hands up and ask sharply, "Why do we keep talking about this?" To my chagrin, what I found out was that listing off all my reasons for *not* wanting a treadmill conversely led my husband to think that I would really *like* a treadmill, and I was trying to convince myself otherwise. Knowing me as he does, he thought I was trying to save money, and he continued to bring it up to assure me that it would be all right for me to have one if that's what I truly wanted.

And there you have it: no amount of best intentions and decades of knowing each other were enough to avoid misunderstanding. The treadmill conversation kept being replayed because he wanted me to have what I might want, and I had sacrificed **clarity** by overexplaining and justifying my position. Too many words—way too many extra, unnecessary words—only created confusion and frustration, while keeping us on this conversation merry-go-round of indecision.

How to Be Brief

A **simple** strategy promotes better communication: craft shorter messages, specifically focusing on the first four words. For instance, I could have said simply at the outset, "Treadmill? No, thank you." Or "Please, no home treadmill." Or "No treadmill for us," Or "I don't like treadmills." Or "I don't want one." Or "Let's not get one." I could have put forth my point of view in so many ways, but instead, I was focusing on trying to avoid sounding blunt or overly assertive. But, with fewer words, I would have made my position much clearer.

Would four words have been the complete conversation between us regarding the treadmill conversation? No doubt there would be more to talk about, but the direction of the conversation would have been so much clearer for both of us if I had talked less and offered more certainty about what I wanted. As a result, my first four words would have signaled to Warner that the task at hand was either to agree or persuade me otherwise. Instead, our respective frustration mounted as we danced around what we thought the other person wanted.

Too Many Words at Work

We see this same dynamic in workplaces. One of my clients, Farah, explained that she had an employee, Ned, who was not meeting performance objectives. As Ned's manager, it was her responsibility to provide him with information about his performance. Farah and Ned met regularly, and when Ned's performance didn't improve sufficiently, Farah put Ned on a performance improvement plan.

Each week, over three or four months, Farah provided Ned feedback about his performance. She regretted doing so, because it was so personally uncomfortable for her, but explained to Ned that he would be terminated if his performance did not substantially improve. Ned said he understood, signed the requisite documentation of each meeting, but because he never improved, Farah decided that she would need to terminate Ned's employment. When Farah told Ned of her decision, he remained sitting in front of her. Perplexed, Farah asked if Ned heard what she'd said. Ned said he did and explained that he was waiting to hear where he would be reassigned. While she thought she was reassigning him to a future employer, *he* expected from their past discussions that he would be offered an alternate position.

Looking back on their previous interactions, Farah realized that she had sorely diminished the impact of her message by apologizing for her dissatisfaction with his performance and by overexplaining why he needed to change. Ned understood her unhappiness with his performance; he just didn't understand the severity of his deficiencies. Farah had so softened her message that Ned, a man in his first corporate position who spoke English as a second language, failed to grasp that his job was at risk. Ned believed that if things didn't work out in Farah's group, there would be other positions that would be a better fit for his abilities.

Ultimately, Ned was fired. But he's not the only casualty in this story. Farah felt terrible and questioned whether she should continue in management. How might this situation have gone differently if she'd had a few **simple**, clear, and ready phrases to use in her conversations with Ned?

- *Your performance must improve.*
- *There is no reassignment.*
- *Your employment will end.*
- *You cannot work here.*

Would he have performed differently if he truly understood that his job was at stake and reassignment was not an option? Perhaps not. But the burden my client felt as a result of the employee's confusion weighed heavily on her heart as she replayed all the ways she could have handled these exchanges more effectively. With clearer and more timely feedback, she could have perhaps helped her employee improve his performance and, subsequently, retain his job for the benefit of himself and his family.

The Significance of Four Words

By now, you may be wondering why not shoot for two words, if being succinct is the ultimate goal. For instance, "Hell, no!" or "No way!" are pretty clear when announcing one's disagreement. A single terse word or two can seem aggressive, impatient, imperious; brusqueness may come off as too commanding.

Certainly, there are times when "Yes" or "No" are sufficient, but often the one-word reply fails to communicate full attention or interest in a topic. For example, a colleague, Anne, explained that she and her husband had constant friction between them. He tended to ask a lot of questions that Anne found annoying. He would ask her something, and Anne, explaining that she was a native New Yorker, said her tendency was to answer with as few words as possible. To Anne's irritation, whatever her response, her husband usually had even more questions in follow-up to what she regarded as an unambiguous response.

I asked Anne whether her terse responses may have left her husband wondering whether he'd made himself clear. Could it be, I probed, that he was understanding her "yes" to mean that she wasn't listening or didn't care?

As Anne considered this, she acknowledged that was probably the case given the kinds of follow-up questions he asked. Though this had been their marital dynamic for years, I suggested to Anne that she try expanding with just a few more words. She started responding with four words instead of one. Here are some phrases I suggested she try:

- *That sounds really good.*
- *I like your ideas.*
- *I think I understand.*
- *Let's talk about more.*
- *What are our options?*
- *Yes, I definitely agree.*

When she took the time to connect with her husband by responding with as few as three or four more words in her response, her husband had more confidence in being heard and understood. Immediately, she reported, it caused a meaningful shift in their dynamic. And it was **simple**.

Other Contexts for "Four"

Four words, as a strategy, came to me through my observation, client work, and conversations with family and friends. Seeing how effective four words could be, I dove into the meaning of the number four. I was struck by how many ways the number four is referenced in nature, music, religion, and pop culture. For one, Don Miguel Ruiz wrote a bestseller, *The Four Agreements*, which he described as the key to personal freedom. Just for fun, here are some examples of what I found:

- In numerology, four represents stability, balance, and completeness.
- Most buildings and rooms have four corners, and four walls.
- Four signifies a strong foundation; there are four sides to a square, rectangle, and parallelogram.
- Navigationally, there are four directions: north, south, east, and west.
- The year is made up of four seasons: spring, summer, fall, and winter. The moon has four phases, and leap year happens every four years.
- There are four elements: fire, wind, water, and earth.
- Humans have four states: physical, mental, emotional, and spiritual bodies.
- In pop culture, we have the Fab Four (the Beatles), and there are four Hogwarts houses in the Harry Potter series.

Finally, with some small bit of editorial license, I quote Winston Churchill: "Keep calm, carry on."

Four Words Is about Possibility and Momentum

As interesting as all of this is, the real significance, though, in finding four words to **start** a conversation has nothing to do with any historical or cultural factoid. Rather, it's in the ability of four words to bridge the space between sitting on the proverbial couch and taking action on what you want to achieve. Knowing how to ask for what you want moves you from "Why bother?" to "Why not?" Think of "four words" as your **minimum viable product**—it's your personal **MVP** for getting things started with minimal effort and stress.

Reframe your thinking when it comes to initiating a conversation and view it as a puzzle to solve instead of a daunting task. This just might change how you view your exchanges at home and in the workplace. The process of coming up with some viable four-word phrases suitable to the situation at hand redirects your thinking and requires you to be creative and adaptive. Instead of anticipating the worst case, your brain begins to react as though it were at play, solving a puzzle.[3] Neuroscientists refer to this expanding flexibility in our brains as neuroplasticity.[4] As you consider solutions from different angles and perspectives, you become more competent, creative, and confident.

---

3 "Why We Enjoy Puzzles: The View from Play Studies," *Psychology Today*, last modified March 2022, https://www.psychologytoday.com/us/blog/the-pathways-experience/202203/why-we-enjoy-puzzles-the-view-from-play-studies.; Mind Tools Content Team, "Solve These Puzzles for Fun, or Work on Them to Improve Creative Problem Solving," Mind Tools Blog, July 5, 2022, https://www.mindtools.com/blog/solve-these-puzzles/.; Chris Griffiths, *The Creative Thinking Handbook: Your Step-by-Step Guide to Problem Solving in Business* (London: Kogan Page, 2016).

4 "Neuroplasticity," *Psychology Today*, accessed February 9, 2024, https://www.psychologytoday.com/us/basics/neuroplasticity.; "Neuroplasticity," Wikipedia, last modified February 7, 2023, https://en.wikipedia.org/wiki/Neuroplasticity.

Try This

Take a look at the following scenarios. What are some four-word phrases you can think of that might be useful in beginning a conversation to address the situation? Feel free to make notes here in this book.

1. You have an employee on your team who is not meeting performance expectations. Your goal is to provide accurate feedback and help them understand how to be more successful in their current role.
2. You learn that one of your customers is dissatisfied with the service she received from your company. You decide to contact her directly.
3. You learn of a promotion opportunity for which you want to apply, but you're uncertain about whether you would be a good candidate for the position. Your initial reaction is to not apply, but after considering it more, you decide to reach out to the hiring manager.
4. Your ten-year-old child describes that he is being bullied by other students at school. You previously spoke with your son's teacher about this, and the problem persists. You decide to escalate the issue by speaking with the principal.

Reflect

As you consider situations that prompt you to want to interact with someone, you may come up with effective phrases that turn out to be five or six words, and that's fine. I want to challenge you, though, to stay curious and discover how much momentum you can create with as few as four words. We'll keep exploring this throughout the book. The goal here is to make it easier to get out of your own way and achieve better results through engaging with people in productive ways.

Jot down some four-word phrases that you want to experiment with to start conversations. As you test these out, notice which work well and which you may want to tweak to improve your results. I encourage you to come back and continue to cultivate this list. You may want to break your phrases into categories, similar to what you'll find in the way that I've grouped phrases by topics throughout this book. You'll find a space like this for you to annotate with your own phrases at the end of each chapter.

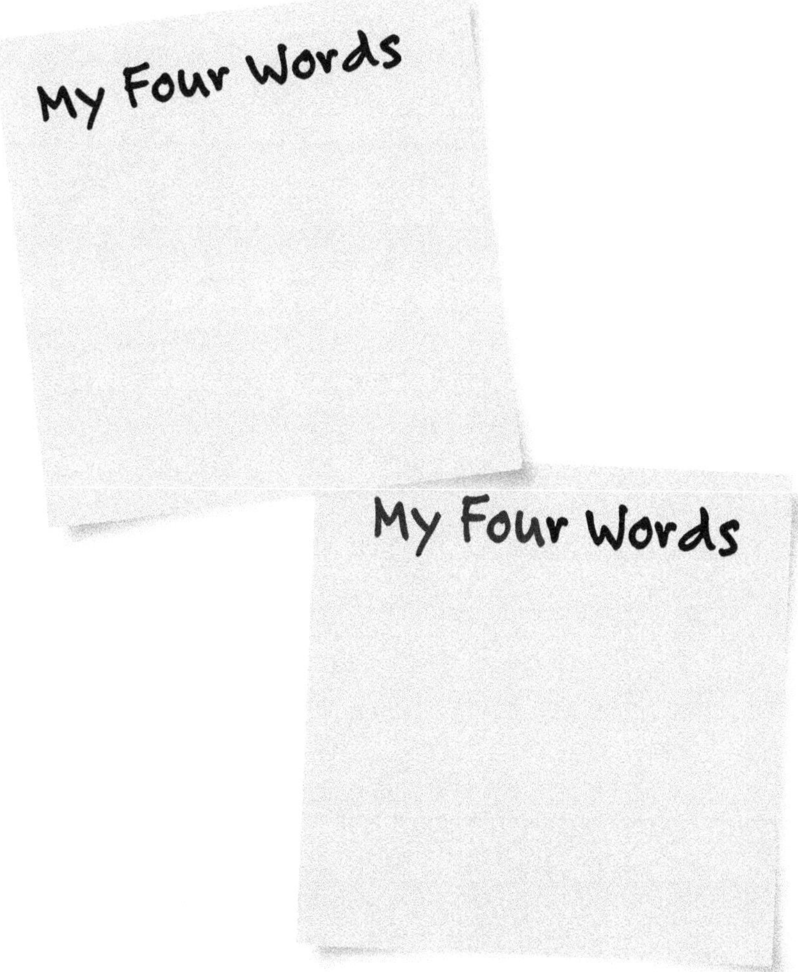

two

four words for four of the most important conversations a leader will have

Four Words at a Glance

- *How can I help?*
- *You have my trust.*
- *We are a team.*
- *We can fix this.*
- *Thank you; well done.*
- *Here's what I see.*
- *What do you think?*
- *Here's what must change.*
- *Let's find a solution.*
- *Let's work this out.*

Why Do People Avoid Conversations?

In my thirty years of working with leaders in various capacities, I've concluded that most problems stem and fester when conversations are avoided and truths are not told. Case in point: I was facilitating a conversation with C-suite leaders of a Fortune 100 company when I heard this:

"But what should I say?" I turned to look at Hans, the CEO of a Fortune 50 company.

"What do you mean?" I asked.

Hans replied, "I know this is a conversation I should have. I just don't know what to say."

Around the room, his colleagues nodded in agreement. And there it was. When faced with having a conversation that everyone agreed was worth having, Hans, like many leaders I've encountered, defaulted to inaction by convincing himself he didn't know what to say. Hans isn't alone in this response. Rather than admitting discomfort, I frequently observe leaders resisting uncomfortable conversations and rationalizing why they don't happen by saying things like:

- *I don't know what to say.*
- *What if I make things worse?*
- *This isn't really my thing.*
- *Others do this better than me.*
- *I always mess these things up.*

It's easy to understand why this happens. The gap between how leaders want to show up and where they feel equipped to show up well, especially when the **stakes are high** and others are watching, often represents a significant risk to their careers or the organizations for which they work.

What's at stake when a conversation goes awry? Your **credibility**, trust, loyalty, engagement, morale, and more. Valued people may leave, performance may decline, or worse. We've all witnessed careers derailed by conversations that became fodder for unwanted headlines and legal actions. These are the reasons that run through the minds of leaders and drive them to justify why it might be best not to have the conversation at all.

This is a very slippery place for leaders to find their footing. Do they risk an uncomfortable conversation or walk away? When conflict arises, do they dismiss it or solve it? It's these moments that test us the most, and without a strategy to lean into, it is far too easy to step away and leave behind interpersonal frictions and misunderstandings that create a substantial drag on intended results.

I've spent a lot of my career trying to sell leaders on why it's important to engage in conversation, making it a point to highlight the impact of shying away and pretending that things will sort themselves on their own. But, as with Hans, agreeing about the value of the conversation didn't equate to having the conversation.

What I've discovered through countless interactions with leaders is that the *why* for the conversation is not nearly as challenging as the *how*. To be sure, others have seen that, too, and I acknowledge that there are many conversational models designed to engage in discourse. But anecdotally, leaders are not lacking in concepts or models. Instead, they are seeking simplicity in the middle of their urgently fast-paced lives. Leaders overwhelmed with day-to-day decision-making and hard-driving business strategies require approaches that are **simple** and practical and can be executed with ease and confidence.

A consultant colleague of mine recently arrived for a virtual conference wearing a T-shirt that said, "I can explain everything, but I can't make you understand." While that is essentially true, it aligns with the idea that leaders strive to be understood, especially when it comes to matters of teamwork and performance.

The best leaders engage with their team members regularly. They are accessible, approachable, and intentional about creating times to meet and discuss projects and items of the day. While the specific content and context of these conversations will vary, there are four topics that leaders need to consistently have with their people:

1. Performance: What I require of you to meet or exceed performance expectations for your job.
2. Conduct: How I expect you to behave in the various aspects of fulfilling your job responsibilities.
3. Support: How can I help you? What do you need?
4. Feedback: Here are my observations of what is working, what's not working, and what could be better.

As straightforward as this seems, these conversations fall by the wayside in the face of urgent problems to solve. They also fall by the wayside when things are going well. Leaders may think to themselves, why bring it up if it's not a big issue? By the time it becomes a big issue, the **stakes are high** for both the leader and the employee, and very often there are other team members or stakeholders impacted.

Taking a more proactive approach and planning to regularly have these conversations helps prevent situations from escalating. It can mean the difference between retaining a talented employee and losing them, a cost that is substantial when you consider the time and investment of posting, recruiting, onboarding, and training. But planning for these conversations is only part of the challenge. It's really about having a plan for how to bring these topics up and addressing issues in real time. This is where the four-word strategy can help to simplify the conversations that leaders need to have and so often avoid until they become mission-critical.

The "What versus How" Conundrum

There are two categories of employee success that are important to identify and address individually: performance and conduct. I often refer to this as the "what versus how" conundrum. When it comes to appraisal systems, it is not uncommon for organizations to weigh an individual's performance along these lines:

What results did they achieve *and* what valued characteristics, like integrity or teamwork, were demonstrated in achieving those results?

Managers for a financial services organization I worked with believed strongly that the *ways* in which employees achieved results were nearly on par with the actual results they achieved. However, when a new CEO was brought in, the 60/40 weighting system they had always applied, was tossed aside. He was concerned that people were giving too much priority to "being nice." He wanted to measure performance entirely based on individual results. Succumbing to internal pressure to continue reinforcing standards of conduct as a crucial element of performance, he begrudgingly approved a 90/10 weighting, with only 10 percent of an employee's performance (where it had previously been 40 percent) based on alignment with company values and standards. The result was mixed—there were strong performance results but at the cost of more employee complaints, interpersonal conflicts, and turf wars. In short, they experienced a rapid cultural breakdown by diminishing the emphasis on positive behavioral norms. They eventually recalibrated to a 70/30 system, which encouraged performance and promoted the employee value proposition of this being a good place to work.

With this example in mind, I want to first focus on ways that you can address expectations with your team members.

Performance: "What I Need from You"

In this instance, *what I need from you* is an opportunity to be explicit about your performance expectations. Why are they important? How are they measured? What are the consequences associated with not performing as required? Relying on the job description alone to do the talking for you is a big mistake. Very often the job posting and the job descriptions provide an overview of a position. They are not helpful in describing what you specifically, as the manager, are looking for. There is a fine line to note in all of this—being clear about what you want from your employees is different from being very specific about how you want things to get done. By dictating how you want things done, you will ultimately be perceived as overbearing, dictatorial, or micromanaging.

To avoid being perceived in these ways, leaders tend to soft-pedal asking for what they expect. For example, one law firm that I consulted with expected associates to be physically in the office between the hours of nine and five every day, unless at a court hearing, deposition, or similar. Unfortunately, it was only the partners who understood this expectation. The partners, when hiring the associates, emphasized the benefits of working at their small firm, which included flexible work hours, a relaxed office environment, and substantial autonomy for even the most junior associates. When I was contacted by the partners to help "rein in these millennial attorneys," the partners complained that the associates were frequently absent from the office, choosing instead to work from home and avoid busy commute times by coming in later and leaving earlier. They also complained that several associates violated dress code requirements. When I asked how long this had been going on, they acknowledged that this had been a problem for *years.* Years! This behavior by the associates created conflicts between the partners and the staff and added on significant hours each week—hours that could have otherwise been spent serving their clients. The impacts were multiple—lost revenue, client and staff complaints, turnover, and more.

I learned through talking with partners, staff, and associates that there were few if any consequences of coming in late and not being available. In fact, the associates consistently stated that they believed that they were meeting expectations. Meanwhile, at least one of the partners was seething about the "laziness" of the associates. As he focused on that, he accumulated substantial evidence supplied by cameras installed at the offices (for safety reasons) that, as a collateral benefit, showed when employees came in and left the office, as well as what they were wearing.

I asked the partners, beyond documenting violations, if they did anything else to reinforce their expectations. They acknowledged they were not consistent in how they handled this. That alone is a big issue. Inconsistency is a tremendous source of confusion. Worse, as I heard when I interviewed associates, the partners were aware of inconsistencies in how individual associates had been treated and a few of them attributed the difference in treatment to favoritism and gender disparity.

Despite their dissatisfaction with the associates, the partners feared turnover. After one of the partners shared the amount of time he was spending fielding complaints from staff, we were able to conclude that the lack of expectation setting and honest feedback was costing them well over $500,000 annually, when taking his billing rate into consideration. That's a big number for a small firm. More importantly, it revealed that turnover wasn't as big a problem as they'd thought.

The biggest challenge for this firm was that they would need to turn the proverbial battleship around. Having allowed unwanted behaviors to persist for so long, it was going to take time to reorient what the partners wanted of their associates, which would involve rethinking how they wanted to promote their firm and the benefits associated with working there. It also meant that some people might leave, and the partners needed to shift their beliefs that as dissatisfied as they were with their associates, other viable candidates were scarce. They believed that the problems they were experiencing with their associates were because, as they stated, the younger generation doesn't work hard. Might it be, I posed, that the problems they were facing stemmed from their own leadership?

Moving forward, the partners determined they would communicate more clearly about expectations, develop a plan to reinforce those expectations, and consistently remind staff of the standards. With additional emphasis on **accountability**, they also planned to introduce a program that offers consistent rewards and consequences associated with adherence to stated expectations.

Allowing Frustrations to Fester Creates Bigger Problems Than Poor Performance

Leaders looking to be respected by "being nice" instead of being clear create diminished productivity and teamwork. These "nice" leaders, when driven to frustration, may also start to demonstrate behaviors characteristic of bullies and dictators by yelling and "cracking the whip."

That's what happened in another law firm. The owner, Frank, had become fed up with his associates and their purported "underperformance" that most interactions with associates were punctuated with sharp criticisms and yelling. Jill, one of the associates, told me that Frank provided no mentoring and would rebuff questions by telling even the newest associates to "go figure it out." Frank distrusted the staff and began micromanaging their comings and goings, and the more he tried to seize control through yelling and rigid rules, the more the staff rebelled. Frank became someone to avoid rather than someone to respect or learn from. Jill said the work environment became so oppressive that the associates banded together and staged a mutiny by taking long lunches, coming in late, and refusing to work outside office hours. Things had devolved to a point that no one was invested in trying to work things out. True to form, the situation ended without a conversation. The associates returned from a lunchtime baby shower for a staff member, and each found a memo from Frank on their desk informing them that they were fired effective immediately. As Jill recalled this, she said, "It was both laughable and a relief. We had no respect for the owner, and we were all ready to leave."

Leadership Means Being Clear; Clarity Is Kind

Being clear about what you expect is a gift to your team, as well as to yourself. Your expectations do not need to be set in stone. They often evolve as business needs change and as you assess the performance of individuals on your team. The conversation you have about expectations, then, is one that is both reaffirmed regularly and refined over time. The job description summarizes basic responsibilities and rarely, if ever, provides sufficient insight into what you are looking for from your team. You might think of the job description as the framing for the role and your stated expectations are the finishing touches. In describing your expectations, consider using specific examples of what you do and don't want to see. **Ask questions**, too, to check for understanding. Here are some four-word phrases to consider:

EXPECTATIONS

- *Here's what I expect.*
- *Here's what I need.*
- *How we measure performance.*
- *Let me explain this.*
- *Timeliness is very important.*
- *Never miss a deadline.*
- *Clients always come first.*
- *Bring problems to me.*
- *We solve things together.*

EXAMPLES

- *These things work well.*
- *Here's a good example.*
- *Please avoid doing this.*
- *This doesn't work well.*

ASK

- *Was I sufficiently clear?*
- *Do you have questions?*
- *What did you hear?*
- *Anything I can clarify?*

These phrases will get you started. If what you come up with is more than four words, that's fine. Remember that **brevity** is foundational to **clarity**. Brevity also ensures that there is space in the conversation for your team member to process, reflect, and inquire.

Coaching versus Directing

A common misunderstanding when addressing expectations is whether what is being explained by the manager is a "have to do" or "it sure would be nice if" assumption. In other words, is what you are describing coaching or consequential to continued employment? To that end, when discussing your expectations, clearly identify what is necessary to meet expectations and what you regard to be extra or preferred.

MUST HAVE

- *Minimum requirements are these.*
- *Continued employment requires this.*

WOULD BE NICE

- *I also like this.*
- *I love it when …*

As a final note on expectations, it is important to acknowledge that your employees have their own expectations of you. To understand their expectations, it pays to be proactive by prompting employees to share what's important to them. We'll touch on this more a bit later in this chapter. For now, here are a few questions you might consider to help initiate the start of your employees sharing with you.

- *What are your expectations?*
- *What is working well?*
- *What could be better?*

- *Do you need anything?*
- *Anything I should know?*

Four words are all it takes to open the dialogue. Four words remind you that when talking about your expectations, it is beneficial to be succinct, invite questions, and explore what others expect of you. Not only does this promote **clarity**, but it is also the pathway to being a trusted, well-liked, and respected leader.

Conduct: "The Way We Do Things Here"

The way things get done informs both employee engagement and organizational culture. Organizations often solve this by communicating company values like respect and integrity, and posting these values on their website or splashing them around the office on posters, coffee cups, and presentations. Anyone would be hard-pressed to argue that respect and integrity aren't important, but in terms of day-to-day behavior, what do they really describe? Some organizations avoid listing individual values and simply tell employees to "do the right thing." As good as this sounds, I've seen many issues arise when people were so uncertain about what the right thing was and the consequences of doing the wrong thing, that they simply did nothing.

In a meeting with a Human Resources leader for a Fortune 500 company, I referred to the company's Careers page, which described to potential applicants what they could expect if they were to work there. The company's values were prominent on the page, and I commented, "You have a great culture here—it's all right there in your values: respect, teamwork, collaboration, and service."

I was quickly interrupted by the HR leader. "Hold on, those values are aspirational. That's not how we really are here." The only thing that surprised me by her comment was her honesty. My heart goes out to those poor candidates who read about the values on the company's Career page and believed that's what they could reasonably expect if they got hired.

What If the Problems Aren't Generational?

Companies and leaders often encounter disruptive behaviors that are inconsistent with intended conduct. I hear a variety of explanations for this—*this new generation doesn't get it, rudeness is the new normal, people don't have time to be nice anymore.* When these are the beliefs for why bad behavior continues, it leads people to conclude that this is a problem that cannot be solved. To the contrary, when employees understand what behaviors are expected and which ones could cost them their job or career, it makes a big difference. That's why you, as a leader, are invaluable in articulating the behavior that you expect from your team. This is not a responsibility that should be left to websites and handbooks. You are both the voice and the model for expected cultural norms that establish successful participation in your organization.

I was consulting with a company about a disciplinary matter involving a vice president of a Fortune 500 company who had received complaints from his staff about abusive treatment that included public humiliation, yelling, and berating employees. He had received corrective coaching for similar behaviors several months previous, and despite that, the current complaints suggested that his bad behavior persisted. While investigating the complaints, the vice president explained to HR that he was being "motivational" by encouraging his team to be more productive. In fairness to this vice president, he was behaving in ways that the leaders in his previous organization had behaved, which, in turn, were what he believed led to leadership success. At his current company, he had discovered that his behavior was unacceptable. While disciplinary consequences were being considered, the vice president submitted his resignation. He explained, "If my behavior isn't acceptable here, this isn't the right company for me."

This was a good, but costly, outcome for that company. Had there been more explicit conversations up front in the hiring or onboarding process for this vice president, many unnecessary costs and disruptions could have been avoided.

Certainly, there are those individuals who, even after expectations are discussed, will still misbehave, but in my experience, they are relatively few, especially when the consequences are fully understood. Still, one stands out in my memory: a senior IT professional started with a new company. He relocated his whole family across the country, and within the first month on the job, while on a business trip, he used his company laptop to download pornographic material, lots of it. The employee manual clearly identified this as a terminable offense, and the employee signed the form that he had acknowledged reading the policies. Did he really read the policies? Doubtful. If he did, it was likely cursory. Upon returning from the business trip, he was promptly terminated. I always wondered how he explained it to his family. It was both regrettable and avoidable, but it happened anyway.

I highlight these examples because the failure to be explicit about conduct standards affects far more people than one might initially contemplate. The collateral damage is great, and in the same way, the collateral damage associated with failing to confront behavioral problems can be substantial. Whole cultures within a team or an organization may erode or become toxic.

Self-Awareness: Looking in the Mirror

A Human Resources leader, Julie, contacted me to conduct training for a high-performing team of software developers. This team had been recognized as one of the best; however, their behavior was also noted to be some of the worst. Julie was concerned that some of the team members could be at risk of losing their jobs if they didn't have some coaching and training. She also told me she wasn't the person who could help them. Inadvertently and quite subtly, Julie realized that she had increasingly adopted some of this team's inappropriate behaviors, and she had only became aware of it when HR colleagues from another part of the company called her out for the ways that she was also demonstrating inappropriate behaviors.

It is important to understand that, as a leader, you are modeling to your employees what behaviors you accept. In more ways than you likely imagine, you are coaching and mentoring when your back is turned, when you are speaking "off the record," when you share or laugh at a joke, when you lead a meeting. I advise leaders to imagine they are always on camera, and they are always being observed by employees and colleagues. What you say and do, what you don't say and do—especially at times when others might expect you to intervene, inform those around you of the accepted standards of behavior. So, whether you discuss your expectations or not, note that your actions may speak louder than anything you say.

Communicate Expectations

This is why I encourage you to be proactive and deliberate in specifying what you expect. It will remind you of your own standards, hold you to a higher standard, and establish guidelines that are meaningful to employees in successfully maintaining their jobs and possibly advancing in the company. Beyond "appealing to the better angels" of human nature, I suggest becoming better leaders by being more specific in your interactions with employees. I encourage you to be definitive in both the "big" behavior issues as well as some that may be more characteristic of your preferred team dynamics. Here are some examples to consider:

DESIRED BEHAVIORS

- *Respect looks like this.*
- *Teamwork looks like this.*
- *Here are some examples.*
- *Here's what integrity means.*
- *Your honesty is paramount.*
- *We listen to everyone.*
- *We value all opinions.*
- *Mistake? Tell me immediately.*
- *Together we find solutions.*
- *We solve problems together.*
- *Let's raise the bar.*
- *We can do better.*
- *Speak and act professionally.*
- *Here's what I want.*

GROUND RULES

- *We celebrate our wins.*
- *All ideas are welcome.*
- *We start on time.*
- *We end on time.*
- *We do not interrupt.*
- *We do not yell.*
- *We do not blame.*
- *We do not gossip.*
- *We arrive at decisions.*

PROHIBITED BEHAVIORS

- *These infractions are serious.*
- *You could be fired.*
- *Others have been terminated.*
- *These are not tolerated.*

Support: "How Can I Help?"

Your best conversations as a leader are those where you are listening more than you are talking. Numerous studies have demonstrated that more time spent listening directly relates to leadership effectiveness. It's easier when you focus on building habits that will help reinforce your commitment to listening. For instance, consider ways to eliminate distractions. It's as easy as setting phones aside, closing laptops, or shutting the door. Space for interaction happens immediately when you **ask questions** and allow time for the other person to respond. This simple strategy of asking and pausing communicates respect, interest, sincerity, and **curiosity**. It also allows for the open exchange of ideas.

Questions are also a means to employee engagement. Asking your team members if they have the tools they need to be successful, asking if they have questions about their job, and inquiring as to any challenges they might be facing will help establish trust and rapport. That's a very high ROI for something as simple as allowing time and space in a conversation as opposed to holding forth.

Here are some **simple** questions to consider:

- *How can I help?*
- *Do you need anything?*
- *Do you have questions?*
- *What challenges come up?*
- *How is it going?*
- *What do you enjoy?*
- *What could be better?*
- *How are you doing?*
- *Is anything troubling you?*
- *How are you progressing?*
- *Who'd you meet with?*
- *Have any new prospects?*
- *How did it go?*
- *What is your plan?*
- *Anything else you need?*

Find a few that work for you and learn to use them regularly. By working with a familiar set of questions, employees will become more accustomed to what they should prepare and how best to use the time you have together. After the meeting, take a pause to assess how much of the talking you did as compared to your team member or colleague. Just be curious, and you'll find you get better at this over time. It makes a difference, and others will notice.

Feedback: "Here's What I'm Seeing"

Finally, the last type of conversation is where you provide timely feedback of your observations. I emphasize "timely," because this is a conversation you should be routinely having with employees. Far too often, I have observed leaders waiting until the performance review to tell an employee about problematic behaviors or performance. At that point, with the review documented and becoming a part of the permanent employment record, it allows the employee no opportunity to correct the behavior until the next review period comes around. Worse, the surprise to the employee often leads to feelings of betrayal or distrust that could have been avoided had the leader been more diligent and courageous in dealing with concerns in real time.

As an executive coach, it always surprises me when I'm hired to work with individuals who have received negative performance ratings regarding behaviors that occurred over eighteen months prior. In my coaching work, I usually reserve the first couple of sessions for the coaching candidate to express hurt, anger, frustration, and the like about receiving a poor review they weren't expecting. I also find that in many of these instances, the alleged problem behavior is largely resolved. That's not to say you have nothing else to talk about—in fact, it usually opens a door to new opportunities and expanded development well beyond the scope of the work initially identified. Still, the fractured trust between my coaching client and their leader is a hurdle that will take time to overcome.

Be Proactive

So, leaders, let me encourage you to be proactive. Giving your team members guidance along the way, letting them know the good news and the not-so-good news, helps establish trust and collaboration. You can become a partner in your team's development when they look to you for mentoring and direction. The goal is to help overcome the gap between where they are and where you need them to be to achieve success in their role. You may also help them prepare for the next level of advancement. Moreover, this valuable and simple step can be addressed with a few short phrases that you incorporate in your one-to-one interactions.

- *Here's what I'm seeing.*
- *You do this well.*
- *Here's something I'm hearing.*
- *Would you try this?*
- *Let's figure this out.*

This reminds me of a time when I was waiting with some employees for a meeting of executives to adjourn. We were waiting outside the conference room when the door opened and the executives came filing out. As they noticed one of the individuals I was standing with, there was a flurrying of congratulatory comments and high-fives directed toward him. "Great job," they said. "Keep it up!"

As the executives walked away, the other employee turned to the one who had been celebrated. "What did you do?"

The other smiled and said, "I have no idea, but I hope I keep doing it!"

Just as it's important to be clear about when someone needs to correct course, making sure that people understand what they are doing well is important not only to them individually, but it helps them provide an example of well-regarded performance to others on the team. As Cesar Millan, the celebrated "dog whisperer," might say, "It promotes the overall wisdom of the pack." And it is the result of effective leadership. *Job very well done.*

A Final Note about Tone

Ninety percent of communication is nonverbal. Facial expressions, tone of voice, gestures, stance—all of these combine in ways that augment or detract from the message of words spoken. So, while you focus on what you will say and ask, it's also important to consider the rest of the message you may send without being aware of it.

When I was working in employee relations, an employee came to me about problems she was having with her manager. She was terribly upset and cried throughout the hour we met. I was able to help her, and we resolved the situation. For the life of me, I can't recall any of the specifics of what she said. What I do recall about that meeting, though, was her emotional state and that my large garbage can was completely full of used Kleenex after she left. It's her nonverbals that left a lasting impression on me. I don't recall her pain, but I do recall it was real.

Location, location, location! We hear this from realtors, but it's worth thinking about for leaders as well. I worked with managers who reported they were frustrated by the number of disagreements they had with each other and their employees. I asked them where they were when these conflicts happened. They told me that they were in the shop—this was a "shop" where they ground clay into kitty litter, and it was both dusty and very, very loud. I suggested they try stepping outside when they needed to talk about something. Almost as if by magic, they noticed they could talk with each other, focus on the issues, and solve problems a lot easier. I asked them to notice how different their faces looked when they were yelling. They acknowledged they often looked angry, and when they used hand gestures to clarify their point, it could easily be perceived as added agitation. Simply by moving their conversation to a place where they could hear each other without yelling and gesturing changed everything.

Similarly, it is your responsibility as a leader to find a time and place to have conversations with your team where and when you can be composed and neutral. The goal is to ensure that you are heard. If what people sense from you is high levels of agitation, they are more likely to react to your emotional state than to hear what you are saying. This is especially the case if you cause someone to be publicly humiliated. It's pretty hard to come back from a situation where people feel unsafe or betrayed. More than one person has staged a hasty exit after being treated in this manner by their leader. Who could forget *Jerry McGuire*?

Try This

Let's leave this topic by exploring the impact of tone when stating phrases you might use for the four types of conversations you will have with an employee. Select three to four phrases, including a question, and with a partner, try expressing these phrases using different tone of voice and other nonverbal expressions. Discuss your observations with your partner. What worked? What didn't work? What could escalate the situation? Are there things you could do to neutralize the conversation to keep it focused on what you are saying?

Reflect

- How clear have you been with your team members about what you need from them in terms of their performance and their conduct?
- How could you be more proactive with feedback to help individuals on your team be more successful?
- Are you making time for regular check-ins and conversations with individuals on your team?
- How clear are you regarding what your team expects of you?
    - Is your response based on actual feedback from everyone on your team?
    - If not, what will you do differently?
- **What are some phrases you want to experiment with to explore the four types of conversations covered in this chapter?**

PERFORMANCE DISCUSSIONS

CONDUCT DISCUSSIONS

SUPPORT DISCUSSIONS

FEEDBACK DISCUSSIONS

Four More Words

Jot down some of your favorite four-word **phrases to talk with team members**.

My Four Words

My Four Words

three

four words that build trust

Four Words at a Glance

- *You can speak openly.*
- *We speak the truth.*
- *I'm here to help.*
- *My door's always open.*
- *What's on your mind?*
- *Tell me about it.*
- *I'm here to listen.*
- *We can solve this.*
- *I will follow through.*

Trust speaks to the quality of the relationship between individuals and organizations, and it is an indicator of overall performance. When there is trust, information is shared more easily and problem-solving is done effectively with the help of one another. Workplace cultures that demonstrate high levels of trust get better business results. This has been well-established by Great Place to Work, McKinsey & Co., and Gallup. Studies demonstrate that where there is high trust, companies experience higher levels of productivity and employee engagement, lower turnover, and less absenteeism; and employees report higher levels of satisfaction with their jobs.[5] Trust is about the bottom line. Research demonstrates higher stock market returns for companies where trust is a cornerstone to the culture.[6] Your ability to develop trust is crucial to your success, as well as that of your organization.

Defining Trust

Recognizing the importance of being trustworthy does not guarantee that others will trust you. That's why I frequently talk with leaders about this topic. All readily agree that trust is important. They nod emphatically when we discuss various benefits associated with building trust. These same leaders, when asked to define trust, often respond with blank stares. Supreme Court Justice Stewart famously declared, when declining to offer a definition of "pornography" (in a 1964 concurring opinion about what factors make a movie obscene), "I know it when I see it."[7] Trust works in the same way: we know it when we feel it, even if we can't fully describe it.

---

5 Paul J. Zak, "The Neuroscience of Trust," *Harvard Business Review*, January–February 2017, https://hbr.org/2017/01/the-neuroscience-of-trust.; IESE Business School, "Why Building Trust Benefits Your Company," *Forbes*, January 24, 2023, https://www.forbes.com/sites/iese/2023/01/24/why-building-trust-benefits-your-company/.

6 "The Business Returns on High Trust Work Culture | Great Place to Work," Great Place to Work, accessed February 9, 2024, https://www.greatplacetowork.com/resources/blog/the-business-returns-on-high-trust-work-culture.

7 "I know it when I see it," Wikipedia, last modified January 18, 2023, https://en.wikipedia.org/wiki/I_know_it_when_I_see_it.

Let's invite Merriam-Webster to step in here. Trust is defined as "assured reliance on the character, ability, strength, or truth of someone or something.[8] In leading a team, what it comes down to is how you demonstrate characteristics that instill confidence. Our everyday behavior is what inspires trust, and our **credibility** is one of the most important assets we have, which is why we need to be conscientious in the ways we build and maintain it.

You may be the sole person whom another person trusts. One employee I spoke with described, with bitterness, how he had been subject to a large-scale layoff at his company. He hated how the company communicated the news but confidently turned to his manager for accurate and honest information. She was the only person he trusted. To her credit, when he reached out to her, she was **brave**. She answered his call.

- *Thanks for reaching out.*
- *I understand you're upset.*
- *This is really hard.*
- *How can I help?*
- *I have some contacts.*
- *This wasn't about you.*
- *I believe in you.*
- *You are tremendously talented.*
- *You've done well here.*
- *Every department was affected.*

The biggest mistake is believing that trust happens by happenstance or by virtue of someone's position. To the contrary, trust is built on consistent, courageous actions. Behaving in ways that foster trust requires diligent effort and is more important than ever. Research

8 "Trust," *Merriam-Webster*, accessed February 9, 2024, https://www.merriam-webster.com/dictionary/trust.

reveals that people are less trusting than ever before. Events in recent years demonstrate growing distrust in the economy, elections, media, government, police, politicians, financial institutions and more.[9] Uncertain times breed hesitancy, and leaders looking to build and maintain trust must become increasingly more intentional about how they communicate and engage with people. Words must align with behaviors, and leaders should initiate conversations that afford people with a sense of security and appreciation. It's in actions like these that trust takes root.

Actions That Inspire Trust

Simply telling someone, "trust me," invariably falls short. The statement itself already hints at a lack of trust, one that will not be solved with words alone. As they say, "talk is cheap." The corollary being, "trust is precious." Trust must be earned and perpetually re-earned. If strained or broken, trust may never be repaired and if it *is* rebuilt, it may take a long time, and unfortunately it may never look like what it once did. People might even remain "on alert" or be less inclined to forgive future infractions where trust is tested.

---

9 Pew Research Center, "Public Trust in Government: 1958–2022," last modified September 19, 2023, https://www.pewresearch.org/politics/2023/09/19/public-trust-in-government-1958-2023/.;

Mara Liasson, "Americans Aren't Thrilled with the Government; the Supreme Court Is Just One Example," NPR, May 3, 2023, https://www.npr.org/2023/05/03/1173382045/americans-arent-thrilled-with-the-government-the-supreme-court-is-just-one-examp.;

Megan Brenan, "Americans' Trust in Media Remains Near Record Low," Gallup.com, September 28, 2022, https://news.gallup.com/poll/403166/americans-trust-media-remains-near-record-low.aspx.;

Erica Chenoweth, Lily Wojtowicz, and Maria J. Stephan, "Polarization, Democracy, and Political Violence in the United States: What the Research Says," Carnegie Endowment for International Peace, September 5, 2023, https://carnegieendowment.org/2023/09/05/polarization-democracy-and-political-violence-in-united-states-what-research-says-pub-90457.

I'm recalling a situation where my husband hired a painter. My husband had a positive experience working previously with this particular painter, so our level of trust was high at the start. Arriving home from work after the painter had completed his project, my initial impressions of the paint job were good—things looked fresh. Going down the hall I noticed, though, a spot that hadn't been painted. Oh well, I thought, I can live with that. But then I saw another spot … and another. My trust, where it had initially been high, rapidly deteriorated as I set aside my dinner preparations and began more carefully scanning for other aberrations in the work. I began flagging the hallway walls with dozens of yellow Post-it notes to identify the spots the painter had missed.

Unfortunately, as I have come to learn, we asked him to do one of the hardest things in the painting world—painting "new and preferred" beige over an existing beige. When the paint is wet, it's difficult to see where you've come and gone. Nevertheless, this has stayed with me as an example of human behavior not unlike examples I see in the workplace. When the trust begins to fray or become strained in some way—for example, stretching the truth, withholding information, not keeping promises—people begin to scan for other examples to validate their conclusion that someone isn't trustworthy. "There she goes again," one might conclude, thereby reinforcing the initial thought while piling on additional evidence to validate the perspective that someone is or isn't trustworthy.

That's why it's so important for leaders to be deliberate in building trust through their day-to-day interactions with colleagues and team members. Creating relationships built on trust provides more predictability and psychological safety, both of which are important in times of dynamic change and uncertainty.

Courageous Connection

Developing trust with each other and becoming a leader recognized as trustworthy, requires consistently engaging with people.[10] In *Daring Greatly: How the Courage to Be Vulnerable Transforms the Way We Live, Love, Parent, and Lead*, author Brené Brown describes vulnerability as the "most accurate measure of **courage**."[11] Tapping into collective wisdom of experience, when I ask leaders to recall colleagues they've trusted in the past, they attribute these behaviors to them:

- *Do what you say you will do.*
- *Walk the talk.*
- *Listen.*
- *Demonstrate respect.*
- *Tell the truth, even if it's bad news.*
- *Avoid distractions.*
- *Make eye contact.*
- *Acknowledge the other person's feelings.*
- *Express gratitude for honesty and courage.*
- *Be consistent.*
- *Don't overreact.*
- *Maintain composure.*
- *Celebrate what goes well; don't withhold praise.*
- *Apologize sincerely when a mistake has been made.*

All these behaviors help build trust, especially when they are demonstrated with consistency. Notice, though, that they all have

---

10 Luis Romero, "The Power of Vulnerability in Leadership: Experts Say Authenticity and Honesty Can Move People and Achieve Results," *Forbes*, March 8, 2023, https://www.forbes.com/sites/luisromero/2023/03/08/the-power-of-vulnerability-in-leadership-experts-say-authenticity-and-honesty-can-move-people-and-achieve-results/.

11 Brené Brown. *Daring Greatly: How the Courage to Be Vulnerable Transforms the Way We Live, Love, Parent, and Lead* (New York: Avery, 2012).

at their root a conversation. You build trust by talking and sharing openly and honestly with each other. The more effective the conversation, the greater the trust.

Build Trust by Investing in Relationships

When I ask leaders what their most important asset is, they nearly always identify people as their number one. Your people are important, and they are costly to replace. You want to retain high-performers and develop talent for your organization, not someone else's. Relationships are the glue. Working with people we enjoy and respect is fulfilling and inspires great performance as well as loyalty.

While you may form sufficiently productive relationships as a function of fulfilling your responsibilities, meaningful connection occurs when you take the time to listen and care about what matters to people. Coming out from behind yourself to share personal stories and experiences is powerful. Stories create emotional connections and help you understand perspectives, particularly when you are presented with opposing views. When you open up to share your story, you **inspire** trust by trusting others with your ideas, lessons learned, and even hardships.

A leadership team I was working with had known each other and worked together for eight years. All men, they were collegial; they joked with one another and demonstrated regard for each other's position and expertise. At the start of our full-day meeting, I asked them to work with a partner and identify as many things about themselves that they believed no one else would have in common with them individually.

When we returned to talk as a group, they individually shared what they believed made them different from everyone else. Stunned, in this small group that seemingly knew each other well, they discovered for the first time that:

- Two of them grew up with parents who had serious mental illness.
- Three of them had lost an immediate family member in car accidents.
- Two of them had children with special needs.

We also enjoyed learning that the CEO secretly loved watching rom-coms; another had written a novel and was looking to get it published. Within a relatively few minutes, we had tapped into unknown territory that in eight years of working together they'd never realized. Where they once believed that sharing their personal stories would make them feel disconnected, they were surprised to discover the opposite was true. Reflecting at the end of the day as to what was the most beneficial part of our work together, the realizations and new connections created as a result of this exercise were acknowledged to be the most impactful. They had become a leadership team transformed by vulnerability and trust.

- *Wow, I never knew.*
- *We have some commonalities.*
- *It's not just you.*
- *Thanks for telling us.*
- *I've been there too.*
- *I know that's hard.*
- *I like rom-coms too!*

The Stakes Are High When Trust Is Gone

Trust is one of those intangibles that, when it is present, pays high dividends, but when it's gone, the consequences can be dire. When people don't trust leaders, they tend to act more out of self-interest. For leaders, it means less knowledge sharing, collaboration, and early identification of issues. The absence of trust can signal the end of a career and threaten the well-being of an organization.[12] Starting in 2016, we saw several examples[13] of this when people came forward to report harassment at work in the wake of the #MeToo movement. One of those impacted was Matt Lauer, the face of the *Today Show.*[14] After greeting viewers every morning for eighteen years, Mr. Lauer's career came to a sudden end after he was fired in 2017 for engaging in sexual harassment of a coworker.

Silence is the symptom, not the disease. Silence signals a lack of trust. In my career I have encountered numerous other examples of people refusing to speak up for fear that things would get worse: an anesthesiologist refusing to report plummeting vital signs of a patient during an operation, afraid the cardiac surgeon would become enraged; accountants failing to report red flags in company earnings, because they were afraid of losing their jobs; workers experiencing and observing harassment but not speaking up, because "that's the way things have always been."

As a frequent flier, I recall being particularly alarmed by a news story reporting that airport ground crews in Portland discovered that

---

12 Debra Meyerson, Karl E. Weick, and Roderick M. Kramer, "The Decision to Trust," *Harvard Business Review*, September 2006, https://hbr.org/2006/09/the-decision-to-trust.

13 Ken Thomas. "CEO Departures in 2019 Were Staggering. MeToo Is Partly to Blame—US News & World Report," *US News & World Report*, January 8, 2020, https://www.usnews.com/news/economy/articles/2020-01-08/metoo-contributes-to-2019s-staggering-ceo-departures.

14 "Matt Lauer," Wikipedia, last modified January 7, 2023, https://en.wikipedia.org/wiki/Matt_Lauer#Career_at_NBC_News.

a passenger airplane flying from Seattle had arrived with a gaping hole near the luggage bay. Investigators discovered a ground crew member in Seattle who admitted to causing the hole when the vehicle he was driving collided with the belly of the plane. When asked why he hadn't said anything, he stated he was afraid he'd get in trouble. So, he told no one about the damage, and the plane, loaded with passengers, took off unaware of the potential risk stemming from the damage.

This story makes me wonder if he hadn't been trained properly or if he had an experience with someone who became angry about mistakes. Either way, because this person didn't trust how people would respond, hundreds of lives were at risk. Why do people fail to take action? The answer lies largely in lack of trust and uncertainty in the outcome. Just as people convince themselves that avoiding a conversation might make things go away, people avoid speaking up, because they don't know who to trust to help resolve an issue without putting themselves at greater risk. There may be distrust in individuals or a process, but the uncertainty of what will happen if an issue is raised causes many individuals to keep silent.

These examples are like so many in the news where, after the fact, after an incident has occurred, the question comes down to *who knew what when*? Take a look at some of the top news stories describing things gone wrong. Notice how many of these stories are the result of people knowing or sensing something wasn't right, and they failed to speak up about it. How could the outcomes have been different if the individuals knew they could trust someone who would help resolve the issues earlier?

Accountability Builds Trust

Everyone makes mistakes. As we've seen, not everyone admits to them. When leaders are forthright about mistakes they make, they build trust while modeling what is expected from their teams. Beyond honesty, taking responsibility by apologizing for misunderstandings or negative impacts helps realign focus and promotes greater understanding. It's also easier than you might think.

- *I made a mistake.*
- *I'm sorry this happened.*
- *Please accept my apology.*
- *I've learned my lesson.*
- *This won't happen again.*
- *Let's make this right.*

Don't try to hide your mistakes; they become much harder to resolve over time. Being the first to acknowledge shortcomings or mistakes ensures the greater likelihood that you will experience grace and forgiveness. That's possible when you realize your mistake. At other times, you may learn that someone has a complaint about something you said or did. Taken by surprise, I've seen leaders become defensive, or when a formal complaint is made, they become obsessed with knowing who made the report. These reactions exacerbate issues and undermine the leader's **credibility**.

- *Take some deep breaths.*
- *Trust in the process.*
- *Remain calm and cooperate.*

Rather than being defensive or looking to get even, remain calm and get curious. Ownership requires accepting that the impact of your actions may be different than what you intended. When working one on one with clients who've received difficult feedback about their behavior, I encourage them to consider how this may be happening *for them,* not *to them* or *against them.* Exploring and experimenting ways to improve demonstrates **accountability** and cements the commitment to work toward doing better in the future. This response will also get you noticed, largely because it is so countercultural. I recall a conversation with a chief financial officer that began with me saying, "I've made a mistake." I could see from his response that he was already bracing himself for what was to come next. I surprised him, though, not with more bad news and a problem to solve. Instead, I briefly explained what the mistake was, how I had resolved it, and what steps I had taken to ensure that it would never happen again. The whole conversation took about five minutes. It also won the trust of that leader and saved both of us a lot of time and energy.

- *I made a mistake.*
- *Here is what happened.*
- *It's all resolved now.*
- *I designed a solution.*
- *This won't happen again.*
- *Thanks for trusting me.*

While there are no guarantees people won't take issue with you, you can expect more grace and the opportunity to repair any harm done, if you've already established mutual trust and respect. Working with leaders, I remind them there is no legal requirement that mandates that they be liked and trusted. One leader expressed hesitation about getting to know his employees personally. He noted that with a growing list of topics to avoid at work—political views, reactions to world events, and perceptions of bias and privilege—he was inclined to keep people at arm's distance. That's an individual choice you'll need to make. I suggest, though, that unless you are perfect and intend to be impervious to the feelings of those around you, it is important to invest in getting to know your team and in allowing them to get to know you as well. Sharing interests and experiences create the foundation for friendships and alliances. Keep it **simple**. You need not share your deepest, darkest secrets.

Holding Yourself to Your Highest Standard

One of the best ways to do that is through the day-to-day interactions with your teams. Be both honest and honorable. Don't promise what you can't deliver. For instance, don't promise confidentiality. If you do, you may find yourself at significant risk for conspiring to keep secrets from your organization. Instead, assure everyone that only those who must know will be made aware of particular events.

As to other topics, use your time with team members to reinforce your readiness to listen and help solve issues. Encourage them to speak with you, to report problems, and to have confidence that problems are being resolved.

- *You did what's right.*
- *This is very important.*
- *Thanks for speaking up.*
- *Is there anything else?*
- *I'll touch base soon.*

People who raise concerns or make complaints are consistently fearful of what will happen to them now that they've come forward. While the outcome is initially uncertain, be sure to acknowledge those who come speak with you. They are doing it in spite of their fear—because they want to trust you.

Proactively Communicate

Anticipating where team members may want additional support or information affords you additional opportunity to build trust. It is especially important that you are proactive during times of uncertainty and disruption, to help promote a sense of calm and focus. You can proactively ask people individually or in team settings:

- *What's on your mind?*
- *What do you need?*
- *How can I help?*
- *Do you need more?*

These questions are powerful diagnostics that can provide you both feedback and direction for where you may choose to be more deliberate about sharing information about strategy, process, and decision-making. Importantly, your silence in these times—or your belief that if people are bothered by something they will bring it up—only adds to the stress. Worse, humans will naturally begin crafting a narrative very different from the one you intend and one that may stray far from the facts of the situation. This is where your leadership is needed most—engaging with people, asking questions, listening deeply. Building trust.

When You Can't Be Fully Transparent

While transparency is celebrated, there are some things where discretion is required as a leader. You may be trusted with information that requires careful handling where you cannot share details with your team. Business requirements and compliance standards around stock offerings, mergers and acquisitions, legal proceedings, medical information, layoffs, terminations, and the like may require that you withhold information. But you shouldn't give up on maintaining trust during these times.

Even where you may not be able to provide all the details, consider what you can share. Talk about the decision-making process, performance standards and criteria, applicable procedures, and the like. When there are questions about a team member's behavior or performance, I have found that saying, "Just as I would be discreet in handling sensitive information about you or your performance, I am required to be discreet in this matter." Here are some other phrases you may find useful.

- *I'm here to listen.*
- *You're entitled to ask.*
- *I can't share everything.*
- *I have some limitations.*
- *Still, I'll be honest.*
- *I understand your concerns.*
- *I'm glad you asked.*
- *Here's how we decided.*
- *I'll explain our process.*

Building Trust in a Virtual World

I'm often asked about the means by which leaders engage with their people. Does it have to be face to face? What about email? Or virtual? There are certainly pros with all these approaches, and many may work. No one solution works in all situations. As we increasingly work virtually, face-to-face meetings may not be feasible. When deciding the method to deliver your message, consider the content and the individual. Which means of communicating will allow for interaction and questions? If there is urgency, which will be the most timely?

Learning from others' missteps, putting efficiency ahead of compassion breaks trust and tarnishes reputations. Take layoffs, for instance. As we've seen, laying people off via email or Zoom tends to backfire.[15] The means of delivering the message may overwhelm the content. Former Amazon employee Jennifer Lucas posted a video on TikTok that depicted her discovering, in an email, that she and hundreds of other employees were being laid off.[16] When she posted the video, it went viral. While Amazon's reasons for the layoff may have been warranted, communicating important messages impersonally tends to destroy whatever trust had existed previously. It also attracted negative attention.

Email has its place in building trust, but it is often not the best initial means of communicating. An email message is useful for following up or to provide additional context or details. In this way, an email message from a senior executive or owner can help bolster trust. Use email strategically and keep it professional.

15 Jack Kelly, "CEO Who Fired 900 Employees via a Zoom Video and Called His Employees 'Dumb Dolphins' Had a Mass Layoff—Some Workers Found Out by Seeing Their Bank Account," *Forbes*, March 9, 2022, https://www.forbes.com/sites/jackkelly/2022/03/09/ceo-who-fired-900-employees-via-a-zoom-video-and-called-his-employees-dumb-dolphins-had-a-mass-layoff-some-workers-found-out-by-seeing-their-bank-account/.; Protocol, "Carvana Lays off 2,500 More Employees," *Protocol*, May 10, 2022, https://www.protocol.com/bulletins/carvana-layoffs.

16 Brigit Katz, "Woman Captured the Moment She Laid Off 900 Employees Over Zoom: 'It Wasn't Real Until I Saw My Bank Account Balance," *Yahoo! News*, March 9, 2022, https://news.yahoo.com/woman-captured-moment-she-laid-195216546.html.

Try This

What are some ways you can make yourself more readily available to team members and colleagues? What behaviors communicate that you are trustworthy, approachable, and ready to help?

Additionally, **experiment** with different approaches for communicating with your team members. What do you notice when talking with people individually versus a group? Which messages are best suited for one-on-one conversations? Which work best delivered face to face?

Reflect

Several actions were described in this chapter to help build trust. Which are ones that are meaningful to you? Which will you apply with your team? What other ideas do you have for promoting trust?

When you are approachable and demonstrate that you care and take interest in them, people tend to trust more. Are there people in your life who would benefit from a little more of your time and attention?

Four More Words

Jot down some of your four-word phrases **that help to build trust.**

My Four Words

My Four Words

four

four words to navigate conflict and create consensus

Four Words at a Glance

- *Let's stop admiring problems.*
- *Indecision is too costly.*
- *This must be solved.*
- *What is our objective?*
- *What's our next action?*
- *Let's take another look.*
- *Let's review the facts.*
- *It's time to decide.*
- *We're in this together.*
- *Let's agree to agree.*

Few people enjoy conflict; it's messy and uncomfortable. When disagreements arise, the typical response is to imagine the worst-case scenario. If this is you, you have a lot of evidence to support the belief that "conflict is a bad thing." Our life experiences and the stories we see played out in our communities and in the news demonstrate that there is a lot at stake when conflicts ensue. Relationships break down or are destroyed. Divisions are deepened. People may be incited to mutiny or revolt. Violence erupts. Wars break out.

Dramatic? Sure. Unrealistic? Not entirely. It's no wonder why people seek to avoid conflict, even when the stakes, by comparison, seem relatively small.

The Bright Side of Conflict

The point is that by focusing on fear and discomfort in the face of conflict, you may miss out on the benefits. While you may not seek out conflict, there is value in accepting it as a natural part of the human experience. More than that, by learning to navigate through conflict—as opposed to ignoring it or wishing it away—you may discover yourself becoming more confident in expressing your point of view and asking for what you want. Pushing yourself beyond comfort and trusting yourself to get to the other side of whatever resistance you might encounter from others are empowering.

Recently I discovered a few invoices for my services that were several months overdue. I toyed with writing them off; without effort, the excuses started to churn in my brain: no big deal, I was too busy to take the time to follow up on the invoices; the amounts were relatively small; my clients are good people, I'm sure they didn't mean to overlook the invoices; if I brought this up, they might disagree, and on and on. When I realized what I was doing, I stopped myself. I didn't like what I was doing. I especially didn't like that I was so willing to give up on the value of services I had provided. I determined that, to be paid, I would need to engage with my clients and stop making excuses for myself or them. I'd need to get out of my own way with regard to the hesitation I felt about confronting the fact that they had not paid me.

Applying the principles in this book, I asked myself what four-word phrase could I use with my clients in starting the conversation as well as acknowledging the positive outcome that I envisioned. Here's what I came up with:

- *I have unpaid invoices.*
- *Who can help me?*
- *I can resend them.*
- *Thanks for resolving this.*
- *I appreciate your efforts.*

With these options at the ready, it was easy to initiate the discussion with my clients. Not only were the unpaid invoices resolved, one of the unexpected benefits was that my clients were generous in their appreciation for my services. I also loved the experience of having my own back.

Low-Hanging Fruit Is a Good Place to Practice

These small points of tension and apprehension are all around us, often fueled by the stories we create in our own minds about what will happen if we speak up on our own behalf. Imagine needing to return an item you purchased. In the array of conflicts that you may be confronted with, this isn't all that big of a challenge. You return the item or you don't. But these small everyday issues offer some real-world experiences for practicing resolution skills. What if it were as easy as:

- *I am returning this.*
- *It didn't work out.*
- *I'd like a refund.*
- *I have the receipt.*

When you enter into discussions with a plan instead of a story of how other people will react or what they will think of you, it's much easier to arrive at a resolution. You are paving the way for better results.

Gina, one of my clients, shared that when a waiter serves her a meal different from what she orders, she doesn't send it back, because she doesn't want to upset the waiter or the chef. I challenged her by asking what it would take for her to trust that the staff genuinely wanted her to be satisfied with her dining experience. I quickly learned the real source of Gina's fear of sending the meal back. Her husband, sitting across from her, insisted she stay quiet and just eat what was served; he warned Gina that if she sent her meal back, the staff would probably spit on her food before bringing it out. Speaking up in this instance meant more than Gina asking for what she wanted from the restaurant; it meant taking on her husband. This was a long-standing dynamic that had persisted in their marriage. If she opted to address it, it would likely take a while to communicate the changes she wanted and instill new habits. While there are no guarantees that it will go smoothly, it could start simply.

- *We need to talk.*
- *I'm not staying quiet.*
- *Allow me to speak.*
- *Why are you threatening?*

- *Please listen to me.*
- *Here's what I want.*
- *I trust people here.*
- *I need your support.*
- *Everything will be OK.*

The lessons in this story apply elsewhere. You see, the way you do anything is the way you do everything. As it turns out, the beliefs that were holding Gina back at work were not unlike what she was experiencing over dinner. Gina, a trial attorney by profession, could benefit by practicing how to stand up for herself and navigate conflict, and what better way to do that than to start with facing her husband over a wrong dish served at a restaurant.

Consensus: The Process of Agreeing on a "Good" Outcome

Mediation refers to a formal process for resolving legal disputes without having to go to trial. My experiences as a lawyer handling cases and representing my clients in mediation have left an indelible impression on me in business negotiations and consensus-making. The indicator of a good mediation result was not simply whether it settled the lawsuit. Beyond settling the lawsuit, a good result was one in which both parties leave a little dissatisfied. That seems counterintuitive when we are more accustomed to hearing about lawsuits being won or lost. But mediation involves earnestly working to find that place of "win-win" where both parties maintain a sense of agency in the decision-making and being heard.

The more passionate people are, the harder it is to arrive at a consensus. If you've ever been involved in a negotiation with designers or program developers, you probably know this from experience. In my own experience, settling lawsuits on behalf of my clients was easier than working with colleagues to determine design features, selecting vendor partners, or aligning on the three-year strategic plan.

When resolving lawsuits or business disputes, there is frequently no *one* right answer, and many times there are several people advocating for "their" version of the right answer. As tensions escalate, I acknowledge leaders for having opinions that are 100 percent right—but only in so much as they represent solely their own point of view. Everyone is entitled to their own perspective, but you must allow for the fact that what's right for you is not necessarily the same as for someone else, and they may be just as strident about their view as you are about yours.

Moving beyond conflict means that your goal must shift from being right to seeking what's best. "Right" only gets you so far, especially when people don't agree. The solution to seek is the one that is "best," which can be informed by a variety of factors including resources, timing, and other perspectives. Coming to an agreement about the best solution means letting go of individual viewpoints, or relinquishing them just enough to allow space for other perspectives and information. The best solution is the one that represents a shared point of view, one in which you and others collectively arrive at a "we" point of view.

This perspective requires humility and understanding. Your own point of view, for as clear as it is to you and for as right as it may seem, may not be what's needed when you consider the range of other perspectives, insights, and experiences. That is the benefit of being part of a team or an organization—there is a wealth of knowledge to tap into, provided egos are set aside and leaders decide proactively to lead with humility and respect.

- *Many perspectives, one team.*
- *All ideas are welcome.*
- *We solve issues together.*
- *Clients deserve our best.*
- *How can we improve?*
- *Let's figure this out.*
- *Divisiveness must not persist.*
- *We listen to everyone.*

Imagine the possibilities if you could view conflict as part of the natural order of things, like changes in the weather. Rainy days are not the result of things gone wrong; they just happen. Similarly, when conflicts arise, trust that nothing has gone wrong. Look, instead, for ways to mend hard feelings and create alignment.

In a competitive work environment where people are vying for visibility and position, the temptation for many is to swing for the fences. More than visibility, employees are seeking notoriety—and they don't want to back down.

Mark, a leader with a clear vision of the outcome he wanted, struggled to sway the senior leadership team to his point of view. With every opportunity he had in front of the senior leaders, Mark kept pitching the decision that, to him, would be the home run he was looking for. The problem was that the executives were cautious. Mark was new to the organization, and the leaders were resistant to the changes he wanted to make. The more Mark pressed on them to commit hundreds of thousands of dollars toward his recommended course of action, the more they stood firm. "Not now, Mark," was their consistent refrain.

Lessons from the Notorious RBG

Too much, too soon is what plagued Mark's strategy. While a huge win is fun when it happens and often engenders some immediate enthusiasm and recognition, always striving for the home run disrupts progress. It's in looking for the big win, or fearing the big loss, that organizations get bogged down and fail to execute in ways that are both productive and motivating to teams. Worse, it can lead to treacherous outcomes. Perennially, companies seeking short-term gains fall prey to scandal or bankruptcy, as with the case of Wells Fargo, Lehman Brothers, Washington Mutual, Enron, Volkswagen, and Purdue Pharma—all of which live on in memory long after news headlines have come and gone.

An alternative approach, one which requires deliberate and strategic action, is to focus on making incremental advances toward the goal or resolution that you seek. By looking for small wins in the direction of what you want, you build **credibility** and gain support. Rather than seeking a home run, you are looking to load the bases to be in the best position to score runs when the opportunity presents itself.

US Supreme Court Justice Ruth Bader Ginsburg was a master of this approach, even early in her career before becoming a judge.[17] She masterfully advanced gender equality not by one case, but many cases over time. As an attorney, she argued six times before the US Supreme Court, and winning five of the cases, she helped establish principles of law that laid the foundation for advancing gender equality and

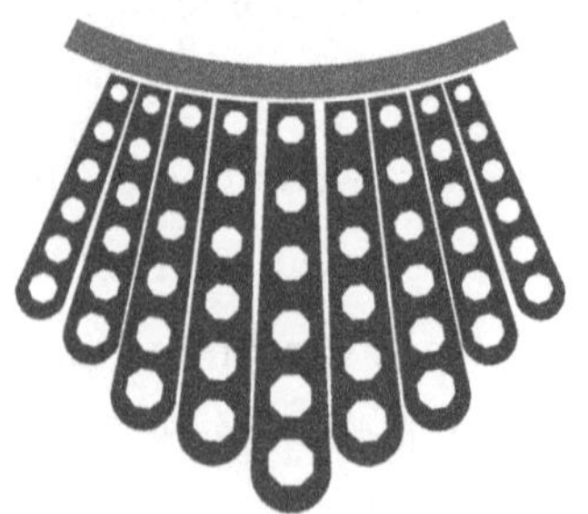

17 "Ruth Bader Ginsburg," Wikipedia, last modified January 19, 2023, https://en.wikipedia.org/wiki/Ruth_Bader_Ginsburg.; Christian Loffredo, "Ruth Bader Ginsburg Leaves Behind a Legal and Cultural Legacy," *BU Today*, September 23, 2020, https://www.bu.edu/articles/2020/ruth-bader-ginsburg/.

rendering sex-based discrimination illegal. Her influence made her notorious. She spoke her mind and built relationships with both those who agreed and disagreed with her. She believed that her adversaries made her better.

That's an important lesson when you think about conflict. So often people are looking to run from it, avoid it at all costs. When you can slow down enough to establish a consensus on the ultimate outcome, it allows more space for different views and also reveals incremental steps toward the goal.

The Pathway to Innovation

Seeking a future solution that improves on the present circumstance is inherently disruptive and requires inspiring others to do things differently, to venture into something entirely new. We have become so accustomed to adapting to technology it's easy to forget how revolutionary iPhones and personal computers were when they first came to the market. The visionaries behind these and other disruptive products were constantly navigating conflicts, both inside and outside of the companies they'd built. Bill Gates, Sarah Blakely, Arianna Huffington, and Steve Jobs—they all had their challengers, and fortunately for those who benefit from their innovations, they had a mindset to overcome naysayers.

When you view conflict as a normal part of the human experience, rather than resist it, you will discover more about yourself and others. Focus on what's working, what's the source of the misunderstanding or the disagreement. By exploring different views and considering dissenting opinions, you may come to understand the underlying issues more deeply, and in doing so, discover new ways of resolving them. Rather than a *breakdown*, conflict may pave the way to your *breakthrough*.

How to Resolve Conflicts

Overall, whether looking for new ideas or harmony, here are four essentials to resolving conflict:

1. **Know the problem to be solved or the outcome you are seeking**. Name it. Don't focus on being right; focus instead on the problem you are looking to solve. This may not end up being the final resolution, but it provides direction and clarifies who you need to engage with.
   - *Here's what I'm seeing.*
   - *We collected some data.*
   - *This needs to change.*
   - *Let's brainstorm some ideas.*
   - *What's a better way?*
   - *Who can help us?*
   - *Who needs to know?*
   - *What resources are required?*

2. **Ask for what you want.** Explain the problem and the rationale for what you are requesting. Allow people to respond with their own words and actions without deciding ahead of time what you think they will say or do. Just simply state what it is you are seeking and allow space for the response.
   - *Here's what I want.*
   - *Here's what I need.*
   - *We all can benefit.*

- *We want the same.*
- *Let's focus on facts.*

3. **Clarify expectations** for how you will engage with each other and what the expectations are once you've arrived at an agreement. One element of this is that you will listen to what others want and need.
    - *Let's set some ground rules.*
    - *We will behave civilly.*
    - *We will be calm.*
    - *Let's take another look.*
    - *Let's review the facts.*
    - *We listen to learn.*
    - *I want to understand.*
    - *Thanks for listening today.*
    - *Let's hear from everyone.*
    - *Let's slow this down.*
    - *Who else can help?*

4. **Confirm what you've resolved to do.** When the meeting is over, don't walk away without reviewing what you've decided. People hear things differently. To avoid making assumptions, talk through what will happen next. Allow questions. Make sure people know what's expected of them and what processes will be in place to keep them on track.
    - *Do we all agree?*
    - *What did we decide?*
    - *Did we overlook anything?*
    - *Are there any questions?*
    - *What's next for us?*

5. **Trust people to do as they have agreed.** For some, this may be the hardest part. But as a leader, it's critical that you know how not only to delegate tasks, but that you also delegate trust. You can still monitor, **ask questions**, and hold others accountable. If all goes as planned, great. If not, then it's time to come back to the table. Talk about what's going on, what's working and not working, and what can be done about it. You essentially will cycle through these four steps again to reach a renewed version of consensus.
   - *Let's keep talking openly.*
   - *Let's touch base regularly.*
   - *How is it going?*
   - *Can we do better?*
   - *Are there new considerations?*
   - *Is there something wrong?*
   - *Shall we meet again?*
   - *What would be better?*

Keep Emotions in Check

Throughout all of these discussions to resolve conflict, tone of voice and other nonverbals, as discussed in previous chapters, are important. Words are best heard when accompanied by kindness, calmness, quiet passion, and truth. These are behaviors rarely celebrated in business, but their power is undeniable. Consider the examples of Mother Theresa, Nelson Mandela, Mahatma Gandhi, Malala Yousafzai, and, yes, Ruth Bader Ginsburg too. You do not need to be someone you are not. You may be more animated by nature, but remember that if the goal is to reach consensus, you should not act as if you are leading a political rally or staging a coup. Keeping emotions in check and demonstrating sincerity, listening, and empathy will go far in helping to reach a meaningful resolution.

When You Can't Agree

Some people are just plain easy to work with. They get you; you think alike; you can finish each other's sentences. But let's be honest, then there's everyone else—and some of those folks are hard to get along with; a few are *really* hard to get along with. It's additionally challenging when they are your boss, clients, or team members.

Don't allow your results or your reputation to be tarnished, because you can't get along with people—even if you believe they are in the wrong. Deeply held beliefs and long-term patterns of behavior are hard to change. If you can't agree on everything, focus on what you can agree on. You may be able to find a path forward despite differing viewpoints. In fact, the more attention you devote to the work at hand and what you acknowledge to be the best outcome, the easier it is to get along. Keep the attention on the project, worry less about the personalities. Decide how you want to perform together well, and to the extent possible, decide ahead of time how disagreements will be resolved when they arise.

Try This

Sometimes you are so close to the conflicts you deal with every day that you begin to accept them as a reality that cannot be changed. To challenge your thinking on this, ask someone to do this exercise with you. Each of you will write down a description of a current point of friction you are experiencing with someone. Then each of you will trade descriptions; you are now holding what your partner wrote, and your partner has what you wrote. Take a couple of minutes to read through what each of you wrote. **Ask questions** to make sure you have a good grasp of the situation.

Now, set the timer for five minutes. Each of you will write down as many four-word phrases as you can think of that might help start and constructively navigate a discussion to resolve the situation that your partner identified.

At the end of the five-minute brainstorming session, share what you came up with. When your partner shares the phrases they came up with, you are to listen without comment. Just consider the ideas. Your partner will do the same. Just listen and consider.

Bonus Exercise

Try role-playing the conversation using one or more of the phrases suggested by your partner. Challenge each other to follow up and try this with the actual person you are in conflict with and agree to share what happens with each other.

It's in doing new things that new space opens up for conflicts to be resolved.

Reflect

What are some "go-to" phrases for you to have ready when conflict arises? Write them down here. As you get a chance to experiment, notice which phrases are particularly useful in getting to consensus. Continue to refine your list based on your experiences.

You might also want to keep track of and reflect on why certain phrases did not work well.

Four More Words

Jot down some of your four-word phrases **that help you navigate conflict and create consensus.**

My Four Words

My Four Words

five

four words that encourage

Four Words at a Glance

- *You can do it.*
- *I think you're great.*
- *I trust you implicitly.*
- *You have something special.*
- *I want to help.*
- *We support you completely.*
- *I know you can.*
- *We believe in you.*

Meeting with the owner of a national training company, we were catching up over a cup of coffee when he was alerted to a text message on his phone. I knew he was expecting news from his sales leader, so I encouraged him to take a look. As we were sitting next to each other at the coffee bar, I looked down to stir my drink, and I saw him type the words, "I'm proud of you." That phrase is my personal kryptonite. There are few things I wouldn't do to hear those words directed at me.

As he turned to explain the message he'd received, I shared how much I admired him for the feedback he had provided. His encouragement of someone else made me appreciate and respect him more.

In contrast, I once worked for a boss who expressed praise by saying, "You haven't disappointed me yet." I knew he meant it to be positive, but it was so backward that it was actually humorous. He just couldn't quite give himself over to saying something **simple** and meaningful.

- *Your performance is outstanding.*
- *You make a difference.*
- *You always come through.*

It's a gift to your team, you, and the entire organization when you are willing to provide authentic encouragement during both the good and bad times. Encouragement is metaphorically like tendons that hold muscles to bone. You can have a talented team and a great mission, but connecting people in ways to flex and perform at their best requires inspiration and encouragement. Don't wait until the performance review to do it. Look for ways to consistently acknowledge people for their contributions.

Encouragement Leads to Strength

Some leaders have expressed reluctance to give accolades for fear that it will make people "needy" or "soft." The CEO of a hospital recently shared that "the younger generation" keeps looking to be rewarded for even the most modest of achievements—like coming to work, being on time, wearing the appropriate dress.

"Have we coddled the younger generation too much?" he asked. "Are we making them weaker?"

I certainly acknowledged that there needs to be performance expectations in place and people should be held accountable; however, it costs nothing for a leader to show appreciation, and that might just be what motivates the employee to come to work. More importantly, what do you gain? Not expressing appreciation for employees is one of the most common reasons people give for leaving their organizations.[18] If you need your employees to help run your organization, try giving them a little extra attention, and see what happens.

Encouragement Can Be Transformative

I was an amateur powerlifter for a few years and competed in a couple of meets. I never planned to get into this—in fact, I'd never heard of powerlifting outside of what I'd seen in the Olympics. It all started for me late one night when I was traveling through Denver and nearly missed my connection home to Seattle. Due to flight delays on the first leg of the trip, I had about twelve minutes to make it to the next gate, and I had to run the entire length of the terminal to get there before the doors closed.

To say I was motivated to get on that plane before the doors shut was an understatement. My children were then in elementary school and too young to be at home alone; my husband's demanding schedule required him to be downtown by early morning. If I missed this flight, not only would I have a long night at the airport, but there was a cascading list of logistical issues that would need to be sorted. Add to that, the fact that it was already nighttime made the logistics even more of a challenge.

---

18 Indeed Career Guide, "Top 10 Reasons Employees Leave: How to Retain Your Top Talent," Indeed, June 24, 2022, https://www.indeed.com/career-advice/career-development/reasons-employees-leave.

So, I did what seemed the only option: I ran. It wasn't pretty. I had on a blazer and heels and was dragging a roller bag behind me. Fueled by fear and adrenaline, I made it with fewer than five minutes to spare. But it didn't stop there. As I heard the airplane doors close, both breathless and sweating with passengers watching, I was then confronted with the task of hoisting my suitcase above my head and into the luggage bin. Somehow, I did it. And then I collapsed in my seat and buckled up. Having made that flight was kind of like those stories you hear about when people, in the face of some disaster, suddenly have a surge of superhuman strength and can pick up a car in time to prevent it from rolling over a small child. I found in myself both speed and strength sufficient to make it home that night and return to all my mom duties the next day.

By way of additional context, let's be clear: I have never been athletic. Far from it. In fact, one friend of mine who runs a minimum of five miles a day often inquired about how I could stand to spend so much time traveling on planes. I would jokingly respond, "Don't underestimate the benefits of a sedentary life." I have countless pairs of socks that I knitted on those flights to prove it.

That night in Denver, though, I decided that I never wanted to question my ability to make a flight or lift my luggage overhead, no matter how heavy. And that's how I found my way to weightlifting. Working with a trainer, my original goal was to lose some weight and gain some strength, and instead, with her encouragement, I discovered the fun of picking up heavy things—really heavy things. My top deadlift weight was 295 pounds. If you wanted your piano moved at that time, I was your gal.

I am no longer powerlifting. That's a story for another day. The point of this story is to demonstrate how powerful words of encouragement can be. In my case, they transformed a previously nonathletic, middle-aged, busy, full-time working mom into an amateur powerlifter and completely changed my perspective on exercise, resilience, and physical strength. I changed, because someone saw something in me, believed in me, and encouraged me to share in a new **vision** for myself. The transformation from breathless passenger to novice weight lifter didn't happen overnight. Instead, it was the result of consistent reassurance.

- *Let's try something new.*
- *I'll show you how.*
- *You can do this.*
- *This will be fun.*
- *You've got this, Tuck.*
- *You're really doing great.*
- *Let's add more weight.*

Of course, it wasn't the words alone that changed me. I had to do the work. I showed up every week, and so did my coach. We did it together, and she supported me in trying things beyond my comfort zone. Over time I experienced evidence that confirmed I could really do this. With her encouragement, I also competed a couple of times and accepted the arduous task of squeezing into a very unstylish and unforgiving "singlet" (a type of compression unitard required at competitions). I was still a busy middle-aged mom through all of this, but I also grew to see myself as strong and athletic.

Encouragement by Any Other Name

Call it encouragement, call it kindness, compassion, or empathy. When you extend generosity to your team members and share the value you see in them, you are offering a gift to them and you. Studies show that well-being is enhanced when you demonstrate kindness. One of the "happiness hormones," oxytocin, is released when you are helpful to others. With little investment of time or effort, you can have a significant impact on yourself and the team. Kindness promotes trust, safety, and connection. Using encouraging words to deliver on that is powerful. As the saying goes, people will remember you by how you made them feel more than for anything specific that you've said.

- *You matter to me.*
- *You work really hard.*
- *Your presentation was outstanding.*
- *You deserve a promotion.*
- *Your future is bright.*
- *Your growth is phenomenal.*

Gifts of Confidence

When I end a coaching engagement, one of my standard practices in our last meeting is to offer what I refer to as a "Gift of Confidence." This is my way of sharing with my clients the strengths I've seen revealed throughout our work together. I am always struck by how deeply moving this is for people.

- *You never give up.*
- *You are incredibly brave.*
- *I admire your courage.*

- *You are so wise.*
- *I respect your honesty.*
- *I love your curiosity.*
- *You serve with integrity.*
- *I appreciate your humor.*
- *You're a great leader.*

These are just a few examples of what I've experienced with clients. What I say is specific to the individual and our work together. This is not a place for catchphrases. To be truly encouraging, your words need to be sincere, not canned, and I cannot emphasize this enough. How unique can you be when encouraging others in your life? Let them know that you see them, really see them.

When Times Are Tough

You can **inspire** your team and organization when you are deliberate in recognizing the contributions and potential of the people around you. In an uncertain world, people hunger for individualized, accurate assessments of their strengths and where they can grow. View encouragement as a type of feedback to help develop people. Numerous studies demonstrate that engaged, high-performing teams attribute their relationship with their manager as a key factor in their motivation and loyalty.[19]

Encouragement is most needed when the path forward seems daunting, if not impossible. You rarely need encouragement when the

19 "Employee Loyalty Statistics: 23 Surprising Stats," BetterUp, last modified January 17, 2023, https://www.betterup.com/blog/employee-loyalty.; Gallup, "Engage Your Frontline Managers First," Gallup.com, accessed February 9, 2024, https://www.gallup.com/workplace/395210/engage-frontline-managers.aspx.; Gallup, "Managers Account for 70% of Variance in Employee Engagement," Gallup.com, March 13, 2015, https://news.gallup.com/businessjournal/182792/managers-account-variance-employee-engagement.aspx.

task is easy. Challenges, conflicts, insecurities, uncertainties, fears—these are the telltale signs of when encouragement is needed. These are times when assuring people of support and safety are helpful.

- *We can resolve this.*
- *Please know I understand.*
- *I know it's hard.*
- *Let's talk about it.*
- *Let's do this together.*
- *You are not alone.*
- *I have your back.*

Providing this encouragement instills a standard and models a way of being part of a team.

- *We help each other.*
- *We can all benefit.*
- *Let's find the win.*

It's in these moments of encouraging others, whether individually or as a team, that trust, connection, and commitment deepen and capability expands.

Balancing Feedback with Encouragement

Your employees are on your team because they were selected at some point and seen as offering value. Developing your team and motivating them to find ways to solve problems and perform better is one of your key responsibilities. To do this, you need to provide feedback. Unfortunately, "feedback" is often perceived as a euphemistic term of bad news: here's what needs to change; here's where you can improve. Balance your feedback by noting what is working well. Let people know you see both the value they bring as an individual and the ways they contribute. Make good news part of your feedback process, and share it often.

- *Here's what I'm seeing.*
- *You really impress me.*
- *You have great potential.*
- *What do you want?*
- *What's next for you?*

You may be thinking, *I just don't have the time.* You've got lots on your plate, and you are sandwiched between the needs of your leaders, your team, your family, and your community. That's why finding **simple** ways to connect through a few reassuring, inspiring, and encouraging words is so important. Because humans are conditioned to avoid perceived dangers, they tend to hang on to the negative information and miss the positive. That's normal. It's commonly suggested that for any one negative comment, it takes five to six positive comments to overcome it. Dr. John Gottman refers to this, in research of married couples, as the "magic ratio."[20] Subsequent studies demonstrated that this ratio is consistent for work relationships as well.[21] So find the time. Encouraging is critical to performance.

---

20 David Mountain, "The Ideal Praise-to-Criticism Ratio," *Harvard Business Review*, March 15, 2013, https://hbr.org/2013/03/the-ideal-praise-to-criticism.; Praiseworthy, "Harvard Research Finds Employees Need a 6:1 Positive Feedback Ratio to Perform Their Best," Medium, June 26, 2019, https://medium.com/@Praiseworthy/harvard-research-finds-employees-need-a-6-1-positive-feedback-ratio-to-perform-their-best-8f14160a8fbd.

21 Marni Jacobs, "The Gottman Ratio for Happy Relationships at Work," *Psychology Today*, June 20, 2022, https://www.psychologytoday.com/us/blog/curating-your-life/202206/the-gottman-ratio-happy-relationships-work.

View Encouragement as a Deliberate Practice

It's a useful practice to reflect on what you appreciate about people—and to do this on your own when they are not sitting in front of you. Find a quiet place, bring a pen and paper, slow down, breathe, and bring the individual to mind. What do you appreciate about them? Jot down what comes up for you. Everyone has strengths. In this moment, even if your relationship with this person is strained in some way, take this moment and see what comes up that you admire or appreciate. If you get stuck, try to imagine what their children or partner may see in them. This simple practice can net tremendous insights and results. It is a first step to providing authentic encouragement. You're building on strengths and potential that you see in the other person—even those folks who get under your skin.

Appreciate Sincerely, Don't Manipulate

Encouraging others is different from cheerleading. As you invest time to focus on what you sincerely appreciate about others, notice how different this is from thinking about ways to cajole people into behaving differently or working harder. For instance, imagine being behind on your revenue goal, and you need your sales team to work harder. Telling the team they are great and you are certain they can increase their sales volume by 50 percent in the last quarter is not encouraging. At its worst, it is self-serving and manipulative, unless you have reason to genuinely believe that each person can do that and you are willing to help them get there.

Discovering Yourself as You Encourage Others

Words of encouragement have the ability to take us well beyond ourselves, surpassing where you are and where you imagine you might go. You, as a leader, have the same ability to affect the lives of others. Not everyone will respond in the same way. Some will soar. Others may draw comfort from your reassurance.

You may also be surprised that one of the people who benefits the most from you giving words of encouragement is *you*. When you step back to honestly take stock, some of your most challenging people may have characteristics you appreciate, ones that you may even want to celebrate or nurture. This in itself may completely transform your relationship with the person or expand how you see them.

This is what happened for the manager of one of my clients, Noelle. Noelle was told by her manager that she needed to work on her executive presence. I asked her for specifics. She said she didn't know any; she didn't have an example of what her manager was concerned about. When I suggested that Noelle explore this more specifically with her boss, she said it would be too uncomfortable. She explained that she had heard the comment about her lack of executive presence long enough and nodded when her boss brought it up. It would be too embarrassing for her to express uncertainty this late in the game.

I suggested to Noelle that we have a conversation with her boss so that we could explore this further. Being a relative newcomer to the story, it was easy for me to ask for specifics. "What do you mean by 'executive presence'?" I asked the manager. "Would you provide examples?" He provided a clear definition with examples to illustrate what he meant. I took notes. Then, one by one, I asked the manager, with my client also listening, to please provide specific observations for each identified example of executive presence of where my client was deficient. Ultimately, working our way down the list, the manager came to the realization that over the previous several months, Noelle had in fact—almost to his surprise—demonstrated excellent skill in each of the areas he attributed to executive presence. His acknowledgment of Noelle's contributions shifted his perspective about her. As a postscript, she was promoted two months later.

You Have More Time Than You Think

Spend part of your day giving back to your team. If you can take time out of your day to order a sixteen-ounce pumpkin spice grande oat milk latte, extra hot with light whip, then I'm confident you have someone in your immediate sphere who you can impact with a few encouraging words. You might even find the experience to be addictive. They deserve your gift of confidence, and you may discover that by modeling this behavior, they'll have some well-deserved encouraging words for you as well.

Try This

We all experience significant milestones in life and work where we are beginning a new chapter (and often closing another). In these new experiences, a few encouraging words may help people feel more welcome, confident, or optimistic. On your own or with others, brainstorm some of these milestones.

Here are some potential milestones to get you started:

- *Graduating from college*
- *First day at a new job*
- *Promotion from team member to manager*

- *First day at a new school*
- *Buying a house*
- *Having a baby*
- *Starting a business*
- *Competing in an athletic event for the first time*

For each milestone that you come up with, what are some four-word phrases of authentic, genuine encouragement? If you are working with a team or a partner, try some of your phrases out on each other and provide feedback.

Reflect

Setbacks are another type of milestone that are part of the human experience. Think about a setback or two you've had in your life. It may have been an unexpected illness, someone passing away, or being laid off or terminated from a job. When you've had an experience like this, can you recall examples of encouragement you received from others? Was it easy or hard to accept encouragement? What helped? What did you learn from these times? For example, one of my readers shared that her dad encouraged her during the hard times by saying, "Keep your chin up." Used one time, that phrase might not be all that impactful, but for them it had become their own language of encouragement in the face of difficulties.

Four More Words

Jot down some of your four-word phrases **to encourage others.**

My Four Words

My Four Words

six

four words to navigate a networking event

Four Words at a Glance

- *Let's see what happens!*
- *This might be fun.*
- *I like meeting people.*
- *I'm learning new things.*
- *I'm open and optimistic.*
- *I prepared some questions.*
- *I will be curious.*
- *It will get easier.*
- *I'll get through this.*
- *Let's just be ourselves.*
- *We can go together.*

Networking events are nearly as varied as the people who attend them. They span across different levels of formality and can be anything from a casual meetup to more formal gatherings that require memberships and criteria for joining. A networking event by any other name is still an event where people come together and exchange information to explore the **possibility** of helping one another or supporting a common cause.

These gatherings sound simple enough and are filled with opportunity; however, I rarely meet anyone who gets excited about attending them. Most people have a love-hate relationship with networking; networking is fraught with unknowns that leave many feeling uncertain and vulnerable. Who will I meet? Will I like them? Will they like me? Will I say something I shouldn't? Will I be dressed appropriately?

What If Networking Could Be Fun?

Last week, while I was at an informal networking gathering, I was chatting with four other women business owners. I shared that I was writing a chapter about networking for my book, and I asked them what their first thought was when they heard the word "networking." It didn't take long for them to respond. Without missing a beat, their answers started rolling in. "Annoying mingling, repetitive small talk, bad news for introverts, salesy, too many people talking about themselves, too much pressure to talk about myself and keep people engaged." Only one person, not surprisingly the woman who organized our gathering, had a positive response; she described networking as "productive socializing." She went on to explain that as a solopreneur working out of her home, she relished the opportunity to get out of the house and connect with others in her community.

By the end of the night, we all agreed that the gathering was a success. We had fun and learned a lot about each other. Some of us shared the same quirks: two of us discovered that we organize the apps on our phones in an identical rainbow order. We also learned that we knew many of the same people, and we all shared a love for New Orleans and dogs. One woman also had us in suspense when she announced, "I have two sugar gliders that live with me." We braced ourselves for where that comment was going, and we were both relieved and intrigued to learn that these tiny marsupials made good pets. (Look them up. They're cute.)

Networking Is Important

Like most things in life, if you focus on your discomfort instead of the benefits, you will miss its importance. Worse, you may convince yourself to avoid it all together. Networking is important, though; it's a powerful way to build connections. You network to learn about others and allow them to get to know you. This is invaluable whether you own a business, have a sales position, or are working in a corporate setting. The relationships established through networking are important for building more connections, creating and expanding your business, and gaining access to useful information. Equally important, interacting with others at networking events, and in general, is a means for building trust and sharing connectivity among the people you come to know. Besides, the more you practice, the better you get at it. Your discomfort subsides, and you may find yourself actually enjoying your interactions.

Not everyone you meet will become a close connection. Theoretically, the maximum number of friends and acquaintances that you can sustain social connections with is around 150.[22] That is not to say that you should look to acquire this many connections and then stop.

---

22 "Dunbar's number," Wikipedia, last modified January 27, 2023, https://en.wikipedia.org/wiki/Dunbar%27s_number.

Our networks, as with those of others, are constantly changing. You will have some people who are migratory or tourists, camping out in your world for only a time. Others may become longtime residents in your network. Your objective should be to surround yourself with people who you find helpful, uplifting, grounding, insightful, and more—and you should be able to offer something to them as well. Your willingness to allow others the chance to help you is often all they want. That, and your appreciation. Just don't take advantage of it.

Curiosity and Experimentation Are the Keys to Success

Even if you're eager to see people you know, there is still the pressure of having to give that thirty-second introduction. Then there is the dreaded small talk. Personally, I can go deep all day, but spending ten minutes on small talk is exhausting, and well, really boring. But let's stop right there. That is exactly the kind of mindset that limits opportunities and connection.

If you imagine that a networking event requires you to spend two hours asking strangers the same questions ("What do you do?," "Where are you from?," "How long have you been there?"), it's going to be difficult to get excited about attending the event. Allow me to propose some alternative ways to view networking. What if conversations with new people didn't have to be boring? Are there questions you could pose that would go deeper than the perfunctory single-word response? Instead of eliciting a ho-hum answer about the weather or a standard reply about what people do for a living, how might you spark a conversation that reveals some common ground? What questions could you ask to learn more about what people value and how they like to spend their time? A valuable exchange at a networking event lies just on the other side of some thoughtful, easy questions.

With these thoughts in mind, suddenly networking became my laboratory. It helped me discover ways to support my coaching clients and help them move beyond the resistance to networking. Better questions helped them switch their internal narrative around so they saw it as an opportunity to learn and potentially advance their career or their business, instead of a burdensome requirement.

Job One: Overcome Your Resistance

What you say to yourself before a networking event may be one of the most important skills to master. This is a time to confront your excuses and get out of your own way. Focus on the benefits of going to the event and decide what you hope to get out of the experience. You might even invite someone to go with you. Here are some things to consider as you prepare to get out there and start mingling.

- *I'll learn something new.*
- *Introverts can mingle too!*
- *I can be myself.*
- *No one will die.*
- *I might have fun.*
- *This is good practice.*

You can also invite someone to come along with you. You might even make it a competition: Which of you gives out or collects the most business cards? Make it fun.

- *Want to come along?*
- *We can go together!*

- *I'll meet you there.*
- *How about dinner first?*

Lower the Stakes: Coffee Chats, Happy Hours, and Shared Rides

Networking happens naturally wherever people gather. For as much as processes and roles inform workplace interactions in formal meetings and events, other gathering places will organically rise among colleagues. Smoking areas, van pools, and softball teams often provide both community and little clouds of insight as connections and information are shared through these more informal interactions. It's in these relaxed settings that resistance to networking subsides. The walls between work groups tend to dissolve in the break areas where people gather.

I was contacted by another coach who said she was helping some clients with career transition, but they were unwilling to do anything different. She asked if I had some tips on how to get them "unstuck." I suggested she encourage them to have some "coffee chats" with people they already knew, with the purpose of talking about their interest in alternative careers. This tactic presents the opportunity to introduce themselves in new ways, as persons in transition, with people they already know and feel comfortable with. It's still networking. This approach lowers the pressure and allows them to practice skills even while they are trying to determine what they want to do in their careers.

Most Strangers Don't Bite

Networking by any other name is still networking. Conversations can begin as simply as turning to someone next to you and asking,

"Are you heading home?," "What's your dog's name?," "How does this work?," or commenting on a book someone is reading, "I read that too." I tend to favor questions at networking events that lend themselves to more than a single-word response. If you're on a flight, and you're testing the mood of someone you'll be sitting next to for many hours, these simple questions can be a good way to make an initial overture. Or not. It's always your choice.

I shudder as I write this, because this was the same advice my dad gave me when I was in school. I grew up in a military family, and we were always moving. It was so hard to make new friends. My dad would tell me to just stick out my hand and introduce myself. I was ten. And thirteen. And fourteen. Hate to tell you, Dad, that's not the way kids connect. But it does come straight out of the adult playbook. Especially now. People are hungry for connection. You may be too. Networking is key to memories and community.

There was a time when I spent 70 percent of my time traveling. I rarely had long conversations with people I met on flights, but some of the connections I made from a simple comment were remarkable and often profoundly life affirming. When buckled in next to strangers for several hours, I wasn't seeking business opportunities. Instead, I allowed my natural love of learning and my genuine interest in people to shine through. I routinely found myself connecting with others through their stories, many of which I still carry with me today. When these stories come up in conversation with my colleagues, I'm often met with their chagrin for talking with others on plane rides. They simply don't believe it can be beneficial or enjoyable. To them I respond, "You're missing out!" Here are just a few examples:

- One woman I met was a jewelry manufacturer and insisted that I accept hundreds of dollars of jewelry she made. Of course I objected, but ultimately she won out, and I accepted her generous gifts. I love wearing the necklace and ring she gave me, and I think of her and her generosity every time I wear them.
- I enjoyed talking with a former Washington state governor and asked her why she wasn't sitting in first class. Adding to my admiration for her, she responded that as a public servant, she wanted to be where most of the people were. As we deplaned, she also introduced me to the then-president of Alaska Airlines, who was also sitting in coach across the aisle. As I walked out with him, he explained that he wanted to experience what most customers experience. (I didn't point out that I noticed the flight attendants gave him extra cookies.) Walking through the terminal together, I saw evidence of his leadership as he greeted gate attendants and other Alaska Airlines employees, making eye contact, shaking their hands, and acknowledging many of them by name.
- One man I met owned a small plane. I shared that I was going through a tough time with my then-teenage son who had been depressed, angry, and increasingly distant. The man offered and followed up with me about taking my son and my dad on a flight around Puget Sound.
- I learned about embalming and running a funeral home from another passenger. He answered my questions in graphic detail.
- One woman took her seat next to me and hung up the picture of a child on the seat back in front of her. I commented that I'd never sat next to anyone who had decorated their seat before. Over the next hour or so she shared that the picture

was of her infant son who had died tragically and how her faith and community was helping her through the grief.

- At a hotel in Indiana, I chatted briefly with a man who told me he was from Northern California. Commenting on the several shopping bags he was carrying from a nearby outlet, he explained that everything that he and his family owned had been wiped out by wildfires, and he was picking up needed items while on a business trip. It was riveting to hear him recount his family's escape from their home and the impact it had on them.
- A flight attendant discreetly gave me an unopened bottle of champagne for me to take with me after I had provided him with a list of the best knitting shops in Seattle for him to visit during his two-day stay there before returning to Germany.
- I was invited to try salmon jerky by a fellow passenger from Alaska who explained how his family had caught and prepared it in the same way for generations.
- One woman I met on a flight to Milwaukee that was getting in very late because of numerous delays insisted that she drive me to my hotel because I was unlikely to get a taxi. I told her I had never accepted a ride from another passenger before, and she assured me she had never offered, but we both surprised each other by how natural it seemed, and we did it anyway. I hadn't talked to her since, but I had invited her to an event I was speaking at the next day. When she came, I introduced her to another colleague of mine, which led to mutual business opportunities for both of them.

I share these stories to illustrate that networking, at its heart, is about being open to human connection. Think about some of the people you've met and under what circumstances. I met my husband at a meeting of lawyers interested in helping other lawyers. Neither of us expected to find our soulmate when we signed up, but over thirty years later, we are still together.

Genuine caring and interest in others is all that's required. Having this as your goal may leave a more lasting impression that goes beyond getting a lead on a new job or business opportunity. These interactions help us grow as humans and provide us with insights for the future. You're not signing on for a relationship necessarily; you are opening up to an experience.

You're not signing on for a relationship necessarily; you are opening up to an experience.

Start Networking with People You Know

Opportunities to network abound right at home. For instance, I was surprised when I learned several years after moving to my neighborhood that two of my neighbors had careers in areas similar to mine. Learning that opened new territory for us to expand our connection. An erroneous Amazon delivery that came to my house instead of next door led another neighbor to discover that I was a leadership coach—and that was exactly what she was looking for. We had lived side by side for four years and have Amazon's mistake to thank for both our work together and our friendship.

Some of the people who may be most instrumental to network with just might be the ones that you've known for a long time. You have an opportunity to catch up with each other, and importantly, you can share what's new with you and where you might be looking for advice. Even if you've been out of touch for a long time, it's never too late to circle back and reconnect. Just as your circumstances change over time, likely theirs have too. When reaching out, you have a chance to briefly explain why you'd like to connect.

- *I'm starting a business.*
- *I am in transition.*
- *I'm moving to Portland.*
- *I was just promoted.*
- *I'm planning a sabbatical.*
- *I'm graduating next May.*

And then you can briefly explain why you'd like to talk with them. You may be seeking input, advice, perspective, or help.

- *You give great advice.*
- *I respect your opinion.*
- *I have some questions.*
- *I'd value your perspective.*
- *Would you have suggestions?*
- *Who should I meet?*

One of the benefits of reaching out to dormant contacts is that since you've been out of touch for a while, any spark of a renewed connection is a gain. If they don't respond, you haven't lost anything—as long as you don't take it personally. If you reach out and don't hear back, you can coach yourself:

- *He's probably really busy.*
- *She may be traveling.*
- *Now's not the time.*
- *We'll reconnect another time.*
- *I'll try again later.*
- *It's not about me.*

What may surprise you is how ready people are to meet with you again and how eager they may be to help you out or offer some encouragement. When I was starting my business, I reached out to several people who I had worked with early in my career. Though it had been as much as twenty years since I'd spoken to some of them, I was warmly welcomed to set up calls and we had great conversations, some of them leading to new business relationships.

Nurture and Cultivate Networking

Networking is a means to **start** a relationship, not a means to close a deal or get a promotion immediately. Those results take time and are often the outcome of having established trust and **credibility** first. I was reminded of that recently by someone I met when I was the president of a local networking group. Sal was virtually visiting from another chapter and stayed after the meeting to introduce himself to me and offer some suggestions of things that were working well in their chapter. I appreciated Sal's suggestions and asked to meet with him again. Over the course of the year, Sal and I met about four times over Zoom, talking for at least an hour each time. I also visited his chapter to see him in action as he led the meeting. We connected instantly and in successive conversations we took time to learn about each other's respective businesses. Part of this process was sharing tips on software and marketing, and discussing how we could support each other, taking the time to understand what kind of referrals each of us was seeking. Not only did we cover a lot of ground in those conversations, but we also laughed a lot. Somewhere along the way, we became friends despite living in different states, owning entirely different businesses, and having never met in person. This had all happened when Sal surprised me during our most recent conversation. He said, "I have been doing this a long time, and I have an extensive network of people who I've met, but I'm going to do something I've never done before, Tucker. I'm going to refer my wife to you. I have kept my personal life separate from my business and networking, but as I've come to know you, I think you and my wife could be helpful to each other."

What an honor—and a good reminder that networking is the first step toward building trust. Establishing a relationship is not a one-and-done activity. Your network is invaluable to you and to others, as you never know who is on the other side of a connection. You might be able to introduce someone to their next best referral or help someone land their dream job, and vice versa. Nurture it. You never know where it might lead.

Don't Wait for When You Need a Job or a Referral

There have been times when people have told me that networking is not working for them. They reached out to someone, and nothing happened. Networking is a process, not a transaction. I have multiple clients who have come to me as the result of a referral from a networking partner. In three recent instances, the people who referred new business to me were individuals I had known and stayed in touch with for over twenty years. Importantly, in each of these instances, these were first-time referrals. They hadn't referred anyone to me earlier, because they hadn't identified a potential client who needed my services, and my services had changed during that time. That they could refer business to me now is the result of nurturing my network, one connection at a time.

Networking is often left to job seekers and business owners but is also an important career-building activity that should be attended to regularly. My son was just hired for a data analytics position after several months of being unemployed, because his previous employer went out of business. He lamented that he wasn't as prepared for networking as he would have liked, and had he been a more proactive networker when he was in school, he might not have taken the initial job with the start-up company. Starting this new job, he is committed to actively networking with people to expand his connections and keep abreast of opportunities for advancement. This is an important lesson for him and for all of us. As the pace of disruption increases, you need to be agile and open to new directions.

As the pace of disruption increases, you need to be agile and open to new directions.

You may not get a job because of who you know, but you will likely get some insight that will help you move forward. Consider networking as your ticket to ride. At a minimum, you'll meet new people, and others will have a chance to get to know you. Just don't make it harder than it needs to be. Be honest, raise your hand, and keep it **simple**.

- *Tom, free for lunch?*
- *I'd like to volunteer.*
- *What opportunities are there?*
- *I'd like your insight.*
- *I was laid off.*
- *I'm reconsidering my direction.*
- *What are your thoughts?*
- *How might I start?*
- *Who should I meet?*
- *Anyone who could help?*
- *Anyone who's done this?*

- *Would you introduce me?*
- *Anyone who has experience?*

The Person You May Be Surprised to Meet Could Be You

Opportunities come to people who are known, liked, and trusted. Look for ways to become more visible by participating in groups or volunteering for projects. You may not think of these kinds of activities as "networking," but if they get you out there meeting new people, it counts. Beyond who you meet, you may discover new talents in yourself. The trajectory of my professional life changed after I asked my manager early in my career if I could be assigned as a Loaned Executive to United Way. My company sponsored me to work with United Way on their fall fundraising drive for three months. I discovered a passion for speaking and gained confidence by working with leaders in different business sectors. Returning to my company after my tenure with United Way ended, I enjoyed expanded visibility and had opportunities to take on leadership roles not previously offered to persons with my background.

- *Curiosity is my superpower.*
- *I'm learning new things.*
- *I'll discover something new.*
- *I'm ready for change.*

Networking Online

People are hungry for connection. Look at the success of LinkedIn. Millions of professionals rely on LinkedIn for insight, community, and opportunity. (Feel free to connect with me on LinkedIn, in fact!) Social media developers have made it easy to click on a name and send a connection request. A more meaningful bridge can be made, one that may create a natural opportunity to actually connect with a person instead of their profile, by personalizing the request to connect. This takes a bit more time, but it is good practice for other networking efforts, and it gets easier. You might reference one of their recent posts, some shared connections, similar experiences, or an event you both registered for or attended. This is your opportunity to stand out by having taken the time to learn more about someone else. You'll also be more likely to have your connection request accepted.

- *We share several connections.*
- *We have shared interests.*
- *We're both Eagles fans.*
- *I like your posts.*
- *I value your expertise.*
- *Want to join me?*
- *Interested in learning more?*

Keep your invite to connect **simple** and short. Your goal is to make the connection, so don't ask for an answer that would require a longer response. This is not a time to ask how things are going in their world. That's too random and vague and will likely be disregarded. Effective networking requires taking things one step at a time, particularly when the only connection you have is online. Once the connection is made, if you are looking to engage the person more, you could suggest a brief call or invite them to an event. And if you don't get a response, don't take it personally. You can check back with them in a couple of weeks. If you hear nothing back, just assume they're busy and move on. There's a whole world out there you can connect with, and someone is looking forward to meeting you—they just don't know it yet.

Four More Words for Job Seekers

- *I'm open to volunteering.*
- *How'd you get started?*
- *What should I know?*
- *Do you have internships?*
- *I'm seeking a mentor.*
- *Do you know how?*
- *Do you know anyone?*
- *Anyone who could help?*
- *Anyone who's done this?*
- *Would you introduce me?*

Try This

What are some networking questions that you could prepare ahead of time that would elicit more than a one-word response? The best questions require more than a yes or no response. I encourage you to think of something that invites people to share something about what matters to them instead of asking them what they did last weekend. There are a lot of things you can ask, but as an added challenge, try using the four-word strategy to come up with some questions that would be good conversation starters with someone that you've only just met.

- *How did you learn about this event?*
- *What attracted you to living here in Seattle?*
- *How did you become interested in genealogy?*
- *What was a highlight from your most recent trip?*

- *What problem do you solve for your clients?*

Accepting my own challenge, here are some four-word questions I use in my own networking:

- *What do you do?*
- *How did you start?*
- *What piqued your interest?*
- *Who were your mentors?*
- *Where did you begin?*
- *Was anything particularly hard?*
- *What frustrates your clients?*
- *What differentiates your business?*
- *What's an ideal outcome?*
- *Describe your ideal referral.*

Reflect

How can you briefly describe what you do and make it memorable? For example, rather than sharing your title or a generic description like "I'm a plumber," think of ways to explain what you do that are provocative or clever. A plumber might introduce herself as "a master of flow" or she could say "I make pipe dreams come true." Someone in building security might say, "I'm an expert observer," or "Meet your new gatekeeper."

If you are a leader, how would you describe what you do in a manner that reflects the legacy you want to leave? You need not be restricted to four words, but here are a few examples that might get you started.

- *I model what's possible.*
- *I build great teams.*

- *I cultivate amazing talent.*
- *I inspire top performers.*
- *I motivate outstanding performance.*
- *I will develop tomorrow's leaders.*
- *I resolve challenging problems.*
- *I smooth production processes.*

Four More Words

Jot down some of your four-word phrases t**o navigate a networking event or conversation.**

My Four Words

My Four Words

seven

four words to smooth the next family gathering

Four Words at a Glance

- *We love getting together.*
- *I'm sorry we're late.*
- *Thank you for hosting.*
- *It's time to celebrate!*
- *Wouldn't Grandma love this?*
- *It's been too long.*
- *Let's just have fun.*
- *This is so nice!*
- *I love you, sis.*

The words "family gathering" spark different images and memories for people. Even the happiest of occasions—celebrating birthdays, holidays, retirements, house warmings, or bridal showers—can be quickly derailed by unguarded comments that hit hard in the moment and remain long remembered after the party is over. Despite Hallmark sentiments, it may be more typical to hear comments like these:

- *Pour me a drink.*
- *Let's all get along.*
- *More eating, less bickering.*
- *Who brought the dog?*
- *Better luck next time.*
- *I didn't say that!*
- *Now the baby's crying.*

High expectations for harmony and frivolity, when mixed with longtime relationship patterns and fuzzy personal boundaries, sometimes create an emotional wake consisting of hurt feelings, rifts, or just plain irritation. Where you anticipated joyous connection, you may end up walking on eggshells. In fact, this is such a common occurrence that a family therapist I recently met shared that she was already meeting and preparing family members for navigating landmines associated with the winter holiday season; it was the fifth of October.

Of course, if none of this happens and everyone walks away loving each other more than when they first arrived and the love you have for each other is felt more deeply than before, that's wonderful. If this is how all your family gatherings consistently go, save yourself the trouble and skip this chapter. If, instead, your family gatherings frequently feature interpersonal frictions and hurt feelings, I invite you to read on. Being prepared ahead of time with a few easy phrases to help soothe feelings and redirect conversations gone awry may be just the thing to set things right.

Disruption in the Middle of Frivolity

One of the challenges with family gatherings is that the dynamics change so much over time as people mature and others come in and out of the family flock. Another common rift is that people often hold tight to family traditions when they no longer serve everyone. While it may be hard to change these rituals, there are times when it becomes necessary to maintain the sanity of the family. My extended family has a tradition of going downtown on the day before Christmas to look at the holiday decorations and pick up last-minute items before we gather at a restaurant for a late-afternoon lunch. I was in my teens when we started doing this when there were only five people in my family—my parents, my two younger sisters, and me. Over time we have grown to include brothers- and daughters-in-law, boyfriends and girlfriends, children and grandchildren.

What used to be simple has now grown to a very large group of people caravanning from different locations. While this day remains the most anticipated of days in my family, it's certainly more complicated than it used to be. Even though we are brought together by love, family, and tradition, we can get crosswise with each other as we navigate unstated boundaries and pain points, all of which evolve over time and are often not apparent until we've crossed a line or hurt someone's feelings. In other settings where we might be less sensitive or impulsive, the thin boundaries and shared histories we have with family often mean that we are saying things without filters and occasionally causing unintended harm.

My family and I are not unique in this. One of my clients describes herself as someone who thrives at work in times of ambiguity and uncertainty. That same client, however, experienced significant turmoil in the weeks leading up to her only daughter's wedding. What was supposed to be a joyous occasion was repeatedly punctuated by moments of tension and conflict in the ramp-up to the big day. Expectations, agendas, and logistics were vague; she felt left out of the loop. With a destination wedding, marriage vows, and a reception behind them, my client's experience was more one of relief to have survived and gotten the whole thing over with.

Over time, I anticipate the pain of that event will fade for her. Still, the complexity of family get-togethers—no matter how anticipated—can stir emotions and reveal previously unseen characteristics of people you thought you knew well. For instance, you may think you know the ins and outs of your brother's personality. However, when he shows up at Thanksgiving with the "love of his life" and a ring for her finger, you realize that you may not have known your brother as well as you thought you did. Beyond your own surprise, you then overhear your mother say, "You're going to marry *her*?" And just like that, your Thanksgiving family gathering is transformed into a day of long-remembered infamy. These family dysfunctions and mishaps are frequently featured in entertainment. Movies like *Christmas with the Kranks* and *Father of the Bride* poke fun at these very realistic dynamics, but the real-life drama that ensues is often painful.

So Much Going On All at Once

Things often go awry between family members when they are busy with one thing and not fully attending to what's being said. You know what I mean: food is being prepared, platters are being passed, gifts are being exchanged, long road trips are being endured, the runaway dog is being retrieved. When reacting to one thing, either the tone or the joking remark lands the wrong way, and suddenly there is tension. The person who is the source may be unaware unless they pick up on the chill in the air. A recent disparaging comment by an unnamed family member prompted a few of us to discreetly look around the room to engage eye contact with whoever else caught the remark. While we kept the peace in the moment, it didn't mean that the comment was forgotten, nor was it necessarily forgiven.

In contrast, I did pick up on the chill in the air after our Christmas guests left last year. Sitting down with my daughter and husband that evening, I learned from them that I was "too snippy" and stressed throughout the day. While I was busy hosting and overfunctioning to meet everyone else's needs, I inadvertently caused people to run for cover. Imagine the difference it would have made if we'd had some simple ways to check in with each other in real time, rather than discussing during the holiday post mortem.

- *We can simplify things.*
- *Don't do it all.*
- *How can we help?*
- *What can I do?*
- *I'll do the dishes.*

Happily, despite not using these phrases in the moment, they were helpful to us in planning how our next holiday event would go. We planned ahead, divvied up duties, set expectations, and asked guests to share in the meal preparation. Best part: we all had a great time. Mission accomplished.

Getting selective about what's doable, what can be delegated, where you can say "No" to activities, and how you can create more unhurried, unscheduled time for you and others is important. For one, it gives you extra reserve and makes you more resilient when things come up that might otherwise hurt your feelings. And there are ways that you can manage some of these things in real time on your own. If you are feeling stressed or overwhelmed, recall why family events are important. Remind yourself of why you put effort into coming together.

- *These are good times.*
- *We'll miss this someday.*
- *I will be present.*
- *I'm enjoying this moment.*
- *Let's hang out together.*
- *Let's take a walk.*

Look for what you can treasure and let go of the attachment that it needs to be a certain way. Family gatherings are as unique as the family members that create them. And as your families evolve, allow your traditions to evolve with them.

Setting Boundaries and Adjusting Expectations

Try as you might, you cannot orchestrate everyone's behavior. The surprises that happen at family events are often some of the most treasured memories. My children and I still talk about the year we made Aunt Judy cry by giving her something she really wanted that she thought was out of her reach. She's tough to please sometimes, and that year we hit it out of the park with her first-ever Kindle when Kindles were fresh on the market. We were more surprised by her reaction and what that gift meant to her than she was about the gift.

Nevertheless, not all surprises are fun. You can avoid some issues by being clear about boundaries and expectations. Rather than adapting to the stress of family gatherings by pleasing people, being proactive about how you want the day to go not only helps everyone understand what's expected but also models ways that they can ask for what they want and need. With less concern about how you think people might react to clarifying what you need, just say it simply, kindly, and directly. Your **clarity** helps everyone else understand what's expected of them.

- *Please don't bring Scooby.*
- *Come when you're better.*
- *No, leave it there.*
- *The presents go here.*
- *Kids, wash your hands.*
- *Please bring an appetizer.*

I can already hear you thinking, "But you don't know how it is with my family!" You're right, I don't. I have found, though, having spent thousands of hours consulting with clients, coworkers, and friends, we're more alike than not. Every family has "boundary busters" who don't follow through on agreed expectations.

For instance, I was recently explaining to a friend about a conversation with my parents, both in their eighties, where I asked that they not talk about funeral plans and such in front of their grandkids. The next day when they showed up at our house to visit with my son and his baby, they launched into a discussion about their wills and long-term medical care, should it ever come to that. Predictably, my son was uncomfortable, and I was a bit frustrated, albeit not terribly surprised.

When I shared this story with my friend Kate, she immediately exclaimed, "The same thing happens in my family!" It happens every time her husband and kids go on a family camping trip, accompanied by her dad. Sitting around the campfire, after a couple of beers, Kate's dad begins telling each person which of his personal items he wants them to have *when he dies.* Kate has asked repeatedly for him not to do this in front of his young granddaughters, but he persists. I asked Kate how she handles it with him. "Consistent, gentle reminders to him before the trip," she said. "Persistent and direct reminders when it happens at the campfire," she added. Kate assures her dad that there will be time to talk privately about this the next day, if he wants. Importantly, she remains ready to collect the kids and go do something else, if need be.

Knowing that you retain the right to step away is always an available option.

You need not be at the mercy of those that don't respect your boundaries. Knowing that you retain the right to step away is always an available option. I emphasize this because knowing how to **start** a conversation does not confine you to staying in one that simply isn't working ... even if it's with family members. But before walking away or severing relationships, you might consider ways to reinforce what you want, especially when what you are asking for disrupts patterns of behavior or family dynamics.

- *Let's try that again.*
- *We all love you.*
- *Please don't do that.*
- *It upsets your grandchildren.*
- *You agreed you wouldn't.*
- *Let's talk among ourselves.*
- *I know it's important.*

Here We Go Again

Best intentions do not rule the day when teasing hits a nerve. Humorous comments usually contain an element of truth to them. Even if the intent is just to tease or poke fun, stray comments can cause wounds that may fester long after the gathering. Any of the following phrases sound familiar?

- *So, you're sober now?*
- *You accepted that offer?*
- *You could do better.*
- *Don't be a jerk.*
- *You're still on unemployment?*
- *You paid how much?*
- *Why change your name?*
- *You can't make me.*
- *You shouldn't say that.*
- *Your kid needs manners.*
- *You stole my boyfriend.*
- *She never loved you.*
- *I hate this casserole.*

These are examples of how things **start**. It's not hard to imagine these triggering an ensuing round of hurt feelings and escalating responses. The tendency to try and brush things aside as quickly as possible often aggravates the situation. Just as you can't unring a bell, once the hurt happens, it is not easily dismissed. That's not to say, however, that people don't try. They might respond with something like this:

- *I was only kidding.*
- *You're taking it wrong.*

- *Don't be so sensitive.*
- *You chose to come.*

These responses rarely land well. I have one client who describes himself as "Jersey through and through." I can already hear how he would handle this situation if something he said made someone uncomfortable. "Whoa, forget about it. I was just venting." I also used to have a boss who would simply say, "mea culpa." Only slightly better, another colleague would say, "Let's just agree to move on." Palliative words rarely erase the hurt, and while the harm may not have been intended, the measure of harm is the impact of the other person, even if that person always takes things too personally or is ultra-sensitive. Worse, avoiding **accountability** for harm further diminishes the person who is offended.

This isn't about right or wrong, fair or unfair. It's about how you navigate these events with a little humor, a lot of respect, and loads of love. Remember, we're talking about family here. People who you love and care about. People who will be in our lives for a very long time. Planning ahead, based on your experience and knowledge of your family dynamics, consider ways to keep the doors open for more conversation, rather than shutting them altogether. The goal here is to redirect in the moment and to allow time and space for conversation later—without people on the sidelines.

- *Let's not go there.*
- *Let's agree to disagree.*
- *Let's not get political.*
- *Let's change the subject.*
- *Please stop teasing me.*
- *That's enough for today.*

Redirection and Delay

When a verbal grenade is thrown, think of ways it could be diffused instead of detonated. Pretending that it didn't happen or sweeping issues under the rug isn't the solution. As a strategy, I've found that proactive redirection is effective.

Imagine your Uncle Phil just lobs a wildly inappropriate comment right in the middle of dinner. Or Cousin Vera makes a drunken toast at your nephew's wedding. You might even imagine worse examples from your own experiences. When no one knows what to say, this is an opportunity to redirect with a complete *non sequitur*, one that you have ready but that seems pulled entirely out of the blue. One of my favorites, though admittedly it's not four words, is "Would you believe my sister churns her own butter?" I also recently learned that one of my husband's former college roommates, while they were living together, killed his girlfriend and was arrested for murder. "Did you know that Warner used to live with a murderer?" I'll say. It's a horrible story, but one that definitely redirects the conversation. My follow-up to this comment is that I only learned this about my husband after we'd been together for thirty years, leaving me to wonder in great suspense as to what else he hasn't told me.

With a few ready interventions like these, you may successfully redirect the conversation and completely open up new and previously unexplored stories and memories. Alternatively, you may opt to share something about a recent trip you took or describe a cartoon from the *New Yorker*. Here are a few phrases that help to redirect the conversation.

- *Let's check the score.*
- *Have you tasted these?*
- *Let's play a game.*
- *Time for cards, anyone?*

- *Who made the rolls?*
- *What's for dessert, Nan?*

A Final Note

None of these strategies or comments are intended to avoid a conversation. They are quite simply offered as in-the-moment interventions. When the time is right, when people are sober, when the onlookers have gone home, when everyone is rested, when you aren't talking over crying babies or barking dogs, when the rolls aren't coming out of the oven, and when no one is trying to watch the game on TV, *then* you can have that very important conversation with your loved one. It's worth a try.

Try This

It's not just families where these dynamics happen. Teams comprised of members who have known each other for a long time and enjoy each other's company exhibit some of these family dynamics. Day-to-day interactions, celebrations, and lunchtime conversations that allow for informality and teasing can disrupt harmony in the group.

With your team, brainstorm some agreeable ways for people to "throw a flag on the play." This can be lighthearted but should be understood by all as a time to take a pause and redirect before things get heated. The statement(s) you come up with should be agreed to and understood in the same way by all—but they need not make sense to persons outside your team.

As an example, one team I worked with came up with a phrase that could be used in interdepartmental meetings to alert a colleague when their team member was being too assertive or argumentative.

They agreed on the phrase, "Would you like a Tic-Tac?" as the signal to back up and take a beat. In this way, they shared an alliance without anyone else picking up on their secret code.

Think of phrases that allow you to proactively throw a flag on a potentially divisive or insensitive comment that signals the need to redirect or possibly apologize. Coming up with these ahead of time helps people respond quickly, and when your team identifies and understands these phrases, it can help solidify teamwork and collaboration.

Here are a few to get you started:

- *Let's not go there.*
- *Flag on the play!*
- *Remember our ground rules.*
- *Let's focus on work.*
- *Let's take a beat.*
- *Please accept our apology.*

Reflect

Take some time to recall some of your favorite family gatherings and invite family members to do the same. You may have photos of some of these events. Share with each other the things you enjoy about being together. Ask what did people like, what went well, what would they like to do more of. You might also ask, "If we were to do things differently, what is one thing that you wouldn't want to go without?"

As you reflect on the discussion, are there any changes you want to make for future family gatherings?

Four More Words

Jot down some of your four-word phrases **to smooth a family gathering.**

My Four Words

My Four Words

eight

four words to compassionately respond to hardships, setbacks, and grief

Four Words at a Glance

- *How did it happen?*
- *What was the cause?*
- *Thanks for telling me.*
- *How can I help?*
- *You did your best.*
- *This doesn't define you.*

It's hard to talk about grief, sadness, and death. My neighbor, a minister, attests that it's even hard for her despite her extensive training in grief counseling. Yet, regardless of our discomfort, there is no way around the fact that we are confronted with all sorts of hardships, our own and others'. What are the words to express empathy and caring when people are evicted, laid off, injured, or depressed? Kudos to the makers of sympathy cards—they make a valiant effort at expressing condolence, but have you read any of those lately? I have yet to find one that resonates for whatever the situation. Mass shootings, suicide, war, cancer. How do any of us talk about these things? How can we connect meaningfully and support each other in these times? The short answer is "It depends." Each situation is unique, and the circumstances of the hardship, your relationship to those who are suffering, and how you learn of it are factors that influence your response.

A Personal Example

"Our son died of cancer." I received this message on Facebook from Ken, a longtime friend who I hadn't spoken with in a while. Unfortunately, I only just discovered this message in my Facebook feed. By that time, it was six years after his twenty-seven-year-old son had died of late-stage colon cancer. As heart-wrenching as this news was, it was worsened by the fact that I had never seen the post, and consequently, I didn't respond. Before I knew anything about the Facebook message, a mutual friend reached out a couple years after Ken's son had passed. When she told me what had happened, I was shocked. I was also stunned, because I was under the impression that Ken had never told me. I thought, why had he never told me? We had been good friends. In fact, I was at his house taking care of his then three-year-old daughter when he and his wife went to the hospital for his son's birth.

Emotions continued to run high when I reached out to Ken to express my sadness about his son. I was unprepared for his fury. He was seething when he said, "I sent you a message, and you never bothered to respond." Taken aback, I assured him that if I had received his message, I would have responded. For years I had wondered if he had been confused about sending the message or if he sent it to an outdated email or mobile number. It was an unsolved mystery until a few weeks ago when I randomly scrolled through hundreds of unopened Facebook messages that I had accumulated over the years and discovered his message. He was right. He did send a message; I just didn't see it in the middle of hundreds of other Facebook messages I ignored.

My conversation with Ken about his son's death and all that ensued was rough. The passage of time doesn't solve the problem of not knowing what to say, and in this case, it made it harder to untangle our feelings and find our way back to the friendship we had long enjoyed. We hung in there, though; we were committed. We had shared history; we had love for each other. Our grief wasn't equal, but we shared loss and heartache.

- *Thanks for picking up.*
- *I wish I'd known.*
- *No one told me.*
- *I wouldn't ignore you.*
- *I know you tried.*
- *I'm devastated this happened.*
- *This is so sad.*
- *How is your family?*
- *I'm glad you're OK.*
- *I love you, Ken.*

I wish this had been the only time when the message just didn't come through. A few months ago, I texted the husband of my beloved friend Marla, who was in hospice care. The last time I called her, it was hard for her to talk, so I reached out to her husband to ask if a phone call would be OK. He immediately encouraged me to call, and when I called Marla's number, her husband answered. He asked why I had called on her phone. Confused, I reminded him that he had just encouraged me to call and talk to her. In the ensuing awkwardness, I started to realize what might have happened. He said, "Did I not reach out to you about her passing?" I told him he hadn't, and when I asked when Marla had passed, I was saddened to learn it had been three weeks earlier. Hurriedly, I told him I needed some time to myself and hung up. And then I cried. I was completely without words in the moment, but found them later when I reached out to him again.

Show Up, Don't Turn Away

When you think of what to say in times of hardship and grief, how you learn of events certainly influences what you feel and, consequently, what you say. Your discomfort may justify not having the conversation, but based on personal experience, failing to acknowledge what someone is going through may actually exacerbate the pain or even sever the relationship. When you opt to say nothing because you are feeling uncomfortable, you run the risk of making things worse.

As the mother of a then at-risk teen, I felt incredibly isolated during that time. My son's struggles escalated to where every one of us in our family was struggling. To describe what we were going through as nightmarish would not be an exaggeration. We never knew from one day to the next what was going to happen, and our lives felt out of control. I felt as though I were failing as a mother, not only to my son but also to my preteen daughter.

From a few friends, I received compassion and understanding; others stopped making eye contact and avoided initiating conversations with me. In my suffering, I acknowledge I may not have been particularly friendly at that time and I may have been difficult to approach, but I can't forget how alienated I felt from the network of people I would have expected to support me the most. Perhaps they thought they were being respectful by not asking about my family. Their silence, however, failed to convey respect. Not only did I feel alone, but also it marked the end for many of those relationships.

In contrast, I attended the memorial service of my neighbor Rob. He and his wife had children the same ages as ours. His family was dear to me, and it was heartbreaking to sit with his wife, my friend, as she shared details of Rob's battle with colon cancer and ultimately his passing. When I arrived at the church for the memorial service, his sixteen-year-old daughter walked back to where I was sitting. She was so poised; I was bereft. We hugged.

"I'm glad you came," she said. Profound. **Brave**.

"I wanted to come," I responded. Four words. Enough said.

Those who are struggling or grieving need to know, "I hear you. I see you." Even the touch of a hand or an embrace from someone may be enough to satisfy that need. There is no perfect thing to say to a parent of a child who has committed suicide. Confronted with this situation when a colleague's teenage son took his life, I struggled to find words to say but sent a note to the grieving mother anyway. I did it because I know how painful it is when people look the other way.

Actions May Be Your Best Response

In the face of another's pain, there are a couple of stand-by phrases that are, to me, too frequently used: *Let me know if you need anything.* And, *I'll keep you in my prayers.* I don't want to dispute the value of saying either of these; I've said them myself. The intentions are good, but the first puts the burden on the person who is hurting to reach out and tell you what they need. I'll just say from my experience, that's a lot to ask, especially when it's not all that clear that the person is really offering *to do anything.* The second, though perhaps genuinely sincere, may feel passive to someone who really needs tangible help or someone to talk to. Alternatively, you might consider one of these:

- *I'm bringing dinner over.*
- *Are there any allergies?*
- *When's your doctor's appointment?*
- *Do you need a ride?*
- *I'll come get you.*
- *I'll watch the kids.*
- *I'm great with organizing.*
- *Let me fold laundry.*
- *I'll come get Fluffy.*
- *I know a plumber.*

You may not know the person well enough where either of you would be comfortable with you helping in the home or with kids. What other things might you offer? Could you organize meals to be delivered? One friend shared that after an immediate family member passed away suddenly, her friends coordinated a full week's worth of meals for her family and left it on their doorstep. No one had asked what she or her family wanted. The friends just rallied together and acted on what they knew was needed: this family was going to be both sad and hungry. The friends couldn't solve the sadness, but they knew how to make sure the family had things to eat and didn't have to deal with the additional stress of having to plan or make runs to the store. Long afterward, my friend continues to feel profound gratitude for this thoughtful gesture. She also learned how meaningful this was and has helped to pay it forward for others.

Of course, what you choose to say will be informed by proximity, circumstance, relationships, and the receptiveness of the person you are reaching out to. Still, you may be surprised at the willingness of people to share what's on their hearts if you are willing to pause and listen. My neighbor of several years lives behind me, and we had never met face to face. We'd talked over the fence several times and apologized for the barking of our respective dogs. I knew very little about her or her family, this being compounded initially by work schedules, a tall fence, barking, and then later, COVID-19. A few months ago, though, we surprised each other by both being in the one spot in our backyards that allowed us to see each other face to face. We were both taken aback when it happened and suddenly there we were at last after all these years. In the ensuing half hour after exchanging comments about how the shutdown had affected us, she confided to me how hard it had been raising her teenage son, who is on the spectrum, and required a lot of in-home school and care, so much so that she had to quit her job to attend to the needs of her family. "I'm exhausted," she said. As she talked, I listened and empathized.

- *I've been through similar.*
- *You're doing your best.*
- *It feels lonely, right?*
- *Give me your hand.*
- *May I call you?*
- *How about a walk?*
- *Want to come over?*

And from her, I heard:

- *I needed to talk.*

- *Thank you for listening.*
- *I've been so lonely.*
- *I appreciate your understanding.*

As we said our goodbyes over the fence, while I didn't say this to her, I do keep her in my prayers. *Hang in there, Margo. You'll get through this.*

Compassion Without Judgment

Sometimes the attempt to "keep things light" can be dismissive. Few people need cheering more than they need compassion. I recall when my dad was approached by a staff member at his church who commented that she hadn't seen him in a while. He explained that he hadn't been at church for several weeks, because he had been recovering from quintuple bypass surgery. Standing next to him at the time, I was appalled when she patted his chest and, with a chuckle, said, "You better take care to get more exercise now, Jon." He took her comment in stride. I didn't. I responded to her, "Before you make judgments like that, you might want to ask him how many miles a day he had been walking before this happened." Taken aback, she did ask him and when she heard his response, she apologized and stepped away.

What none of us knew at the time was that this was just the beginning of my dad's serious health issues several years ago. For a while, it seemed that every medical test or appointment revealed another problem—blocked arteries, skin cancer, lymphoma, collapsed lung, pneumonia, blood clot—you name it. We jokingly asked him to quit going to the doctor, because he kept coming back with more bad news and more treatment protocols. We were either going to laugh or cry. Taking cues from my dad, we relied on his and our senses of humor to get through this difficult time. In contrast to the woman at church, our comments were welcomed and lovingly expressed, without judgments or assumptions.

This difficult time for my dad happened over ten years ago, and happily he pulled through. Most people were kind in their comments, though invariably things were said that were hurtful. For example, I cringed when people would hear how he was doing and then ask, "How old is he?" I started sharing that I would answer the question if they really wanted me to, but we would be destined to experience an uncomfortable pause afterward, because his age really didn't matter. The point was that he was suffering and so were all of us who loved him. His age was irrelevant.

Similarly, when my ninety-three-year-old beloved neighbor, Norman, passed away, we were grief-stricken. Sharing with friends about Norman's passing, they invariably would ask how old he was. When I would tell them, their expression was often one of nonchalance, sometimes even quizzical. I said, "Look, just because we can see it coming doesn't mean it's not sad!"

Hardships are a part of our human curriculum. You don't schedule them; they just happen. No amount of anticipation or preparation will ensure that you won't experience pain. Accepting that to be true, rather than resisting it, makes it easier to be present in others' pain whether you have the words or not. Tyler Henry, known to many as "the celebrity psychic," commented during his series on Netflix, "At the end of the day, we're all just walking each other home." Incidentally, my mother declared that she doesn't plan on dying. I didn't want to argue the point with her, that she'd told my daughter and me on numerous occasions which hymns she wants included in her memorial service—to which she added, "If anyone were to come, that is." Of course, we'll be there. We'll be sad. And to my mom's comment that she doesn't plan on dying, I responded to her, "We can all plan on dying someday; we just don't need to put it on our schedule." To which my mom laughingly agreed.

Endings Are a Part of Life and Work

Ultimately, grief is grief. Hard is hard. Like smoke in a jar, pain fills the entirety of available space. Your hard may be different from someone else's. While we all experience pain, our pain is relative and often incomparable. Personally, I don't know how people overcome domestic abuse or the death of a child. At the same time, few would want to trade places with me. It's how we show up in the face of challenges and how we support each other that affords us with meaning and purpose. There's no need to have a perfect script for what to say. Just show up and trust yourself. *Everything will be OK.*

While we often associate grief with the loss of a loved one, there are other types of grief, less tragic, that we cling to. In my executive coaching with clients, I was initially surprised by how frequently unprocessed grief came up as a barrier to moving forward. Being confronted with a setback, receiving difficult feedback, working through reorganization, being reassigned to a place you don't want to go, managing a mutinous team, hearing that you're fired—these events can be painful, even paralyzing at times. The tendency is to want to move as quickly to a future where, in the case of my clients, they imagine the pain will stop.

What they don't realize is that they will take the pain with them. Worse, it may influence their performance in ways they don't intend. No matter how hard or how fast you try to push past sadness, the research confirms that traumatic events impact our physical state. As author and researcher Bessel van der Kolk, MD, says, the body keeps score.[23] Many people report sadness, for example, at the anniversary of a loved one's passing. A colleague recently shared how rushing to get a puppy four days after her family's beloved dog had passed effectively distracted them from the pain of losing their four-legged companion of many years, but a year later, they were confronted with the fact that they had a one-year old dog *and* still hadn't come together as a family to acknowledge and mourn the loss of the previous dog. They thought they had moved on, but the anniversary revealed ways in which they were stuck and still sad.

Processing the grief by slowing down and acknowledging the hurt is the key to moving forward, often rather quickly and to a better future state. As William Bridges pointed out in the bestselling book *Transitions: Making the Most of Change*:[24]

Every beginning begins with an ending.

As you find the words to guide yourself through a transition, think about what makes for a good ending or, as I say to my clients, "What does a 'good goodbye' look like for you?" How do you want to be remembered? Who are the people you want to connect with? You may find inspiration in some of these phrases that I've collected in working with my clients:

- *I'll be leaving soon.*
- *Want to have lunch?*
- *Let's keep in touch.*
- *Thanks for mentoring me.*
- *You're someone I admire.*
- *I've learned a lot.*
- *Thanks for the opportunity.*

---

23 Bessel A. van der Kolk, *The Body Keeps the Score: Brain, Mind, and Body in the Healing of Trauma* (New York: Penguin Books, 2015).

24 William Bridges, *Transitions: Making the Most of Change* (Cambridge, MA: Da Capo Press, 2004).

- *We will meet again.*
- *I appreciate our friendship.*
- *May I call you?*
- *Here's my personal address.*
- *This has been great.*

I realize in the heat of the moment, especially when you are caught off guard or don't like what's happening, any of the phrases I've suggested may seem absurdly Pollyannaish. You may, in the moment, have fantasies of revenge or going out in a blaze of glory. If that's the case, I encourage you to pause. These feelings don't resolve in the blink of any eye. Take as much time as you need to allow the feelings to come up and subside. Keep breathing. Find someone outside of work to talk with. Ask yourself what leaving well could look like. Choose to end on a high note. As your feelings neutralize, you will discover new perspectives and more options than are immediately apparent. These insights will help you take deliberate actions that support your future self and career.

Consider this example from one of my clients, Deb, who was surprised to learn that she was being honored with a significant industry award. It was a big deal. At the time, Deb was angry with her boss and her organization after receiving what she believed to be unjust criticism in recent months. Deb intended for her acceptance speech at the awards banquet to be her opportunity to point out how wrong her leaders were about her, because here she was being recognized by her industry peers for delivering outstanding work.

In the weeks leading up to Deb's speech, we talked about the reputation she wanted to have and the legacy she wanted to leave. As we did so, the acceptance speech seemed less an opportunity for retribution and more of an opportunity to shed light on her personal values, which included thanking people who had a positive impact on her career. In her speech, Deb credited her career mentors and team members, including her current leaders. This was a triumphant night for Deb and marked a turning point in her relationship with her leaders. Taking the time to work through her anger before the event enabled her to be poised and sincere in her comments, not vindictive.

Setbacks Don't Define You Unless You Let Them

Everyone has moments when we're not at our best or when circumstances overwhelm us.

The initial impact of hardships, grief, and setbacks tends to soften with time. Even still, people may sometimes have a difficult time moving forward. You may hold on to regret or shame, you may have a hard time forgiving yourself or others. Unfortunately, many of the limiting beliefs I encounter with clients stem from them hanging on to past experiences and allowing those beliefs to define their future. But take heart, these hardships and setbacks, big and small, need not be the whole story of our lives unless we make it so.

A workshop participant shared this saying with us: "Don't judge the story by the chapter you just walked in on." This goes for the ways that you may judge yourself. Are you being too hard on yourself? If you are having a hard time letting go of what's holding you back, seek help like my client, Colleen, did. Colleen led a team two years before I met her, and her experience with that team was disastrous. The team rallied together against her, and after a tumultuous year of trying to gain their support, Colleen took another assignment. Leaving the team in this way made her feel like a failure. Where she had believed herself to be an excellent leader, she now felt humiliated and was counting down the clock for when she could retire.

In contrast to how Colleen felt about herself, I spoke with her executive leaders. They saw Colleen as being a high-potential leader, but they had seen her shrink away from expanded leadership opportunities after stepping away from her "mutinous team." Rather than seeing the event as a mark on Colleen's competence, the executives admitted that everyone who had ever tried to work with that particular team had experienced similar treatment. The problems were with the team, not Colleen. They also admitted that some of the problems stemmed from the failure of the organization to make more holistic structural changes with regard to the team.

As I worked intensely with Colleen over several months, she came to realize that she was, in fact, valued and competent. She had forgotten about her qualities in the middle of the setback she experienced. Colleen dove into new projects and accepted high-visibility projects—bringing new energy and enthusiasm to them. Meanwhile, others have sought her out as a mentor. In a recent conversation with Colleen, she was preparing to heed the encouragement of senior leaders in her organization and throw her hat in the ring to take on a significantly elevated leadership role. Her future looks bright!

You are not alone in your suffering—while our challenges may be different, the fact that we all have them unites us in this human experience. Your challenges, though unwanted, make you stronger and almost always make you better; don't let them weaken you or define you.

- *It's only a chapter.*
- *I know it's hard.*
- *Things will get better.*
- *You'll get through this.*
- *Let's do this together.*
- *I've been there too.*
- *There's always a way.*

- *Time heals all wounds.*
- *I'm here to help.*

"Life's best lessons are the hard ones," a client told me. So true. View your challenging times as merely a chapter in your story, not your identity. By the same token, as a leader, you may afford the same grace to others, acknowledging their hard chapter and encouraging them to focus on the bigger, better story.

Try This

Working with a partner, share two or three occasions when you didn't know how to respond when something happened to another person in your life. Brainstorm some approaches and come up with three or four four-word phrases that the two of you agree would be helpful to hear if you were in one of these situations yourself. How does it feel when you're the person offering comfort? How does it feel when you are the person being comforted? Share your experiences. Invite your partner to suggest alternatives.

If you learned of a situation in an email or text, consider how you might respond in the email and whether it would be good to follow up in other ways.

Brainstorm other ways to support people going through difficult times.

Reflect

When you've experienced a challenging situation, think about the ways that people responded to you. What helped? What didn't? How do these examples help you determine ways that you do and do not want to respond to people?

Four More Words

Jot down some of your four-word phrases **to respond to heartache and hardships.**

My Four Words

My Four Words

nine

four-word questions to deepen understanding and connection

Four Words at a Glance

- *How did it go?*
- *What was it like?*
- *What was your experience?*
- *Where are we aligned?*
- *What did I miss?*
- *What is your feedback?*

Deepening understanding is the result of inquiry. Asking questions demonstrates respect for others' experiences and points of view. But questions will only take you so far. It's in the listening—without interrupting or hurrying someone along—that understanding and connection take root. For that reason, in this chapter, the focus is on

curiosity, listening, and respect—all of which can be demonstrated with four-word questions and your willingness to listen.

Active listening is a skill, rarely an innate talent. It is also countercultural in many organizations fueled by a sense of urgency, a need for market penetration, and fierce competition. But not listening heightens risk and undermines collaboration. Hurrying people through their story or racing to fix what you perceive to be the problem may actually distract from the real situation requiring your input. You may also miss that a problem came and went; the issue is already resolved, and no one needs anything from you. You are simply being made aware or invited to join the celebration.

During a recent workshop I was facilitating, a senior leader named Frank said, "I know it's important to engage in active listening, but it's so hard." Intrigued by his comment, I immediately asked him to tell me more. Frank explained, "It's difficult to be quiet when I already know the answers." When I challenged him and asked him how certain he was that he knew all the answers, he responded with another objection, "It's too hard to sit still and wait for the other person to finish talking when I have so many other things that have to get done." What Frank had concluded was that with insufficient time to listen, why start a conversation?

The Benefits of Slowing Down

Listening is an intentional act. It involves pausing, concentrating, being still, and not interrupting. And, to Frank's point, it does take time. But, frankly (pun intended), there are so many reasons why conversations are important, especially with team members. Even the most seemingly incidental conversation is part of what forms the bedrock of teamwork and trust.

Failing to step back and slow down may prove incredibly costly. Bob Iger, CEO of Disney, recently acknowledged that results at Disney had floundered in recent years. When asked what happened, he answered—with four words coincidentally: "We lost some focus."[25] Like Disney, Apple and Starbucks have also lost their ways at times. Starbucks, for instance, was once regarded as progressive, in part due to the company culture and treatment of employees, which they referred to as "partners." Times have changed. With growing concerns about wages, scheduling practices, and physical safety, Starbucks partners have been organizing to form unions at individual stores. Unionizing efforts and the NLRB (National Labor Relations Board) involvement have changed public sentiment and led to store closings. As we've seen from other instances, even Starbucks's own examples from previous years show that comebacks are possible. Founder Howard Schultz returned as CEO two times after initially retiring in 2000.[26] But these comebacks don't happen unless you actually *listen* to understand the issues that led to the setback in the first place.

A cancer research organization that I once worked for was recognized for both advancements in cancer treatment and having an outstanding workplace culture. However, the leadership team confided that their single most difficult day-to-day challenge was the disruption caused by fast-moving leaders on a mission to cure cancer who were simultaneously unaware of the impacts of their behavior. Team members reported feeling bruised and distrustful of key leaders because they had been snapped at or publicly humiliated. When leaders were confronted about their brusque behavior, they justified it by attributing time they could have spent "being nice" as coming at the expense

25 Justin Bariso, "Bob Iger: The Key to Handling Too Many Priorities," Inc.com, accessed February 9, 2024, https://www.inc.com/justin-bariso/emotional-intelligence-disney-ceo-bob-iger-how-to-focus.html.

26 "Howard Schultz," Starbucks Stories, accessed February 9, 2024, https://stories.starbucks.com/leadership/howard-schultz/.

of lives lost. What these leaders missed, though, was that being united against a common enemy—in this instance, cancer—affected their ability to slow down and consider the impact of their behavior on valued team members, and was undermining the very innovation and engagement they needed to achieve their goals.

More and more of my clients tell me they are feeling immense pressure to move fast, make quick decisions, and execute swiftly. I recently met with the members of a tech company where they pride themselves on solving problems with laser precision and speed.

"Have you noticed that many of the employee issues your managers experience are the result of moving too quickly?" I asked.

"Yes," they replied. "Our managers may make snap judgments or 'go with their gut,' and then things don't go as well as they hoped." They explained that employee complaints demonstrated the tendency of leaders to "wing it," doing what they thought made sense at the time despite having little knowledge or experience. Compounding problems, these managers failed to coordinate internally with human resources to ensure that decisions were made fairly and in compliance with both legal and company standards. What was supposed to be their market differentiator—speedy action—was creating an unintentional drag on results; their perceived need for speed and execution had inadvertently produced a culture of mavericks who acted on their own without understanding the risks brought about by their actions.

How to Slow Down

These situations aren't uncommon, but they are avoidable. Moving quickly often requires deliberately slowing down. Being proactive in slowing down from time to time may also make it possible to move forward much more efficiently. It is far more difficult—and takes much longer—to turn a ship around after it's gone off course.

Taking time to develop a deep understanding of your business, clients, and team members is critical. You might think of it as shifting down to a lower gear when you are about to drive up a steep hill. Slowing down allows time for emotion to neutralize, facts to be gathered, and strategies to be assessed. It also affords time to communicate, inquire, and inform. Without that, you may lose sight of what is really important, and in return, you'll suffer a loss of focus.

Initiating conversations to examine needs and current realities is a first step to building connection and will expand your knowledge base. Begin with questions. **Ask questions** that invite a story or response. When asking questions, avoid those who can be answered with one word and, instead, allow people to expound and paint a picture.

- *What are you seeing?*
- *Are we off track?*
- *Are we losing focus?*
- *Why aren't folks engaged?*
- *What's slowing us down?*
- *What needs to change?*

These moments of interrogating reality may be the beginning of something important. It's up to you to allow the time and space for this kind of inquiry to happen. Prepare to set your feelings aside. And listen.

Coaching Yourself to Be an Active Listener

Managing competing priorities of listening and doing, you can employ the four-word strategy to help sit with the discomfort of being still. Asking questions demonstrates your commitment to listen and respect others' viewpoints. Coach yourself by silently asking questions like these:

- *Am I really listening?*
- *Am I paying attention?*
- *Are my eyes focused?*
- *Am I taking notes?*
- *Am I responding thoughtfully?*
- *Am I eliminating distractions?*
- *Am I still breathing?*

The only thing you need to do in this moment is listen. Breathe deeply. Relax your face. When you do, you may find that your mouth eases into a gentle smile. These nonverbals will put you and others at ease. You might also remind yourself that, at least for the moment, "There's nothing to fix," "I'm just here listening." You might even consider, "How can I step back, perhaps empower others to handle this?" A vice president of human resources shared this advice with me that she uses with managers: "Facts before freaking out. Let's just stay focused."

Invite Your Challengers to the Table

Your ability to take this time to pause and assimilate the available information is helpful to making better decisions while also conveying sincerity and respect to the person with whom you are speaking. This is the nature of respectful communication, of course. The going back and forth, thoughtfully considering each other's perspective, and responding to concerns as opposed to impulses. It's this dynamic that affords connection and deeper understanding, and even allows for the

possibility that you might respectfully agree to disagree. Abraham Lincoln famously leveraged this approach by establishing his cabinet of adversaries, assembling a team of advisors who had differing views. He wanted to learn from people who thought differently than he did. More than that, through discourse and debate, he wanted to understand their viewpoints. Where there might have been divisiveness, Lincoln inspired trust and admiration. Pulitzer Prize–winning author Doris Kearns Goodwin, author of *Team of Rivals: The Political Genius of Abraham Lincoln*, described Lincoln in a 2006 interview:[27]

> He understood that human relations are at the core of politics and that if you deal with people in the right manner, you are going to be able to work effectively with them. The qualities we associate with human greatness—such as sensitivity, empathy, compassion, kindness, honesty—are also keys to political success.

These qualities are the keys to your success as well. Setting aside your to-do list to hear from your team may, in the end, be the most important decision you can make.

When You Don't Think You Have the Time

In this age of screens, global teams, and virtual meetings, informal opportunities to connect face to face are few. It is more important than ever to be deliberate in creating connections with people—and to do so deliberately. You may wonder if meeting regularly or taking time to inquire about someone's weekend or their kids is a good use of time. Why meet with team members when all you need is an answer to a question that you can send in an email or a text?

---

27 Bruce Watson, "An Interview with John W. Carlin," *Prologue* magazine 38, no. 1 (Spring 2006), https://www.archives.gov/publications/prologue/2006/spring/interview.html.

The most important asset you can share with your team is access to you. People don't leave companies; they leave leaders. By the same token, you can be a leader that people are loyal to and someone they want to emulate. Be that person. Take the time to get to know your team, and let them get to know you.

Team meetings are important, but equally important—if not more so—are the individual meetings you have with your team. Set aside the time. Typically, leaders arrange one-on-one meetings with team members. If you're not doing that now, **start**. Make it a regular calendar appointment. There are, of course, limits to how much time you may have for these meetings despite how important they are. If you don't have the bandwidth to meet with everyone individually, get creative. Consider alternatives—just make sure you don't leave anyone out.

One of my clients, Nina, distinguished herself by being one of the very few executive leaders who made these one-on-one meetings with every one of the people in her organization a priority. She wanted to be known by her team and get to know them personally, so she met with her direct reports weekly and with those who didn't report to her less frequently. Nina wanted her team to have access to her. During these meetings, Nina would ask about their career interests; she took notes. When passing people in the hall, Nina was one of the few senior leaders who was able to greet people by name. As her team grew, though, it became increasingly difficult to meet with everyone individually. Nina considered eliminating the one on ones with all but her direct reports, because she couldn't sustain the number of meetings she'd been having, especially now that her team consisted of over forty people and continued to grow. That just didn't feel right, though. One of the parts of being a leader Nina likes best is leading her team and being a part of their lives. Rather than give up the one on ones with everyone, Nina devised a plan to meet with people in groups of three to five and to meet over lunch, outside of the office. She's now trying this out. Importantly, Nina's story demonstrates her commitment and deliberateness in building relationships with her team.

What could this look like for you? If you are a leader, it's pretty straightforward; you schedule the one on ones and adjust where circumstances require. If your leader isn't meeting regularly with you, then ask, as meetings with your leader are critical to your development and your visibility. People trust those who they know most.

No One Is Talking: Getting Past "Fine" and Other One-Word Responses

What happens when you set aside time to listen to someone, you invite a conversation, and then all you get back is a one-word response? No doubt you've asked someone what's wrong when it was evident something was amiss, and the answer you got was "Nothing." It's all too common that some of the questions we ask tend to shut people down rather than open them up. Ask almost anyone on a Monday morning, "How was your weekend?" and you'll likely hear that it was "Fine." It always seems to be fine. Or "Good." Or just "OK." Instead of having a conversation, these one-word responses turn into perfunctory pleasantries. Worse, that may be the end of the conversation before getting down to business.

The tendency is to throw in the towel when this happens. Don't give up. It takes people different amounts of time to warm up. Whether they share anything personal or not, you can. And you can also adjust your approach by asking questions differently. For instance, "What was the highlight of your weekend?" invites more of a story. From the perspective of starting the conversation, asking a broader question not only enables you to learn more about your colleague but also invites you to respond with reactions or questions. Suddenly, beyond starting a conversation, you are *having* a conversation. More importantly, you are laying a foundation for new or deeper connections.

"There's always room for a story that can transport people to another place."
—J. K. ROWLING

That's the power of slowing down. Not only are you giving space to someone else, but you create the opportunity to find the questions that elicit a meaningful response. The questions you ask have the power to transport you and others to a different place in your work together. It's through stories that we connect and expand our perspectives. These interpersonal connections are the foundations of teamwork, collaboration, engagement, and belonging. Gallup has helped organizations for decades measure employee engagement.[28] Central to their survey work are the twelve questions, or "Q12." One question asks, "Do you have a best friend at work?"[29] Another asks whether an employee's supervisor or someone else at work cares about them as a person. These questions explore feelings, but more than that, they have an impact on leadership **credibility** and the bottom line. Where coworkers feel a sense of collegiality and belonging, they have been shown to be more engaged, more productive, and more innovative.

28 "Q12 Employee Engagement Poll," Gallup.com, accessed February 9, 2024, https://www.gallup.com/q12/.

29 Gallup, "The Importance of Your Best Friend at Work Is Growing," Gallup.com, September 16, 2022, https://www.gallup.com/workplace/397058/increasing-importance-best-friend-work.aspx.

I've learned that people will forget what you said, people will forget what you did, but people will never forget how you made them feel.
—MAYA ANGELOU

Lean into caring. Not only will it support better engagement, but it will afford you mercy and forgiveness in the instance you may make a mistake. A colleague of mine recently confided in me, "Tucker, when you were my manager, you didn't always get it right, but I always knew you cared." In that spirit, we forged an enduring relationship founded on deep respect, admiration, and, over time, love.

What's Love Got to Do with It?

We don't talk about love very often in the context of people we work with, and I'm not suggesting you should start professing love to your team members. For one, you'll make your HR partners very nervous. However, it's the appreciation that we have for each other as humans and coworkers that instills positive experiences at work. Countless clients have described their colleagues as feeling like family. That's high praise, in most cases. To that end, find ways to demonstrate that you care and that you are interested in them. Expressing appreciation is also an excellent way to **start** a conversation.

- *I enjoy working together.*
- *We're a great team.*
- *I'm glad you're here.*
- *I like our debates.*
- *You help me understand.*
- *I value your honesty.*

These statements do more than convey appreciation for each other. They also promote a sense of safety, comradery, and well-being. Incidentally, they also help to motivate good performance.

Engaging Courageously with Your Teams

Attorneys are taught to avoid asking a witness questions at trial for which the attorney doesn't know the answer, whereas the best leaders courageously venture into the unknown every day. What is important for trial attorneys is counterproductive in business, where open and honest input is needed. When meeting with your teams, letting go of controlling the conversation allows others to share their thoughts and ideas. Leaders, this is especially important for you in not only building the trust of your team, but deepening your understanding of what's on their minds so you can act on their ideas and help address their concerns.

Learning to embrace uncertainty with confidence is one of a leader's greatest strengths and a gift to those they lead.

Encouraging people to speak freely, albeit respectfully, without fear, is a first step. You may say a few things at the outset to encourage openness, and you may find it useful to provide additional assurances as the conversation progresses.

- *Let's talk about it.*
- *We'll be brave together.*
- *Please state your mind.*
- *We can speak freely.*
- *We'll hear from everyone.*

- *Please wait your turn.*
- *We need to know.*
- *No one's getting fired.*
- *I take this seriously.*
- *Thanks for sharing this.*
- *Let's figure this out.*

Combining assurances like this with open-ended questions establishes and maintains open, inclusive dialogue. It also takes fortitude. Things might get messy. You might not like the answers to your questions. What comes up may be hard to hear, perhaps even harder to solve. It's in these moments when leaders demonstrate whether they are willing to walk the talk.

It was a meeting like this where my client heard from team members that they were very dissatisfied with their compensation. The employees came to the meeting primed with data; they had researched what people doing similar work in other companies were getting paid, and they asked that their salaries be reevaluated. My client felt blindsided but acknowledged them for being both bold and **brave** in making their request.

- *Thank you for sharing.*
- *Thanks for telling me.*
- *I'm glad we talked.*
- *I agree it's important.*
- *I'll explore this more.*
- *I will follow up.*

More than listening to their request, my client took action. She initiated broader conversation among the leaders in the company regarding competitive and equitable compensation practices. Her goal was to respond to her team's concerns and to also ensure the company would remain an employer of choice in the marketplace.

Conversations with team members also offer an opportunity to reaffirm company commitments to fairness, keeping an open door, and retaining talent. What is important to individuals is often important organizationally. Rather than competing goals, individuals and organizations may share more values than is initially apparent. In workshops, when I ask how leaders want to be treated, their answers are the same as those offered by employees. Too, when we compare those responses to stated company values, there is substantial synergy. Everyone wants the same things, but in the face of day-to-day challenges, sometimes people begin to believe they are at odds. Reminding your team and yourself of fundamental values helps unite each other and focus on solutions instead of breakdowns.

- *We aim for fairness.*
- *We pay people equitably.*
- *You will be heard.*
- *We adjust when needed.*
- *We recognize great talent.*
- *We respect each other.*
- *We are sincerely truthful.*
- *We reward excellent performance.*
- *Everyone's contribution is important.*
- *We keep getting better.*

For leaders, any of these statements may come off as mere platitudes without the actions behind them to make certain people feel heard and valued. To establish the trust of your team, you need to prepare to go to bat for them. Your ability to shoulder the concerns of your team and give them voice with others in your organization is key to both deepening understanding and building trust.

- *Yes, this is important.*
- *I understand your concerns.*
- *We'll look into this.*
- *I'll meet with HR.*
- *I'll follow up soon.*

The answer you bring back to your teams may or may not be what they hoped for, but your willingness to do more than listen speaks volumes beyond anything you might say in the moment. Acknowledge the concern and take action, and follow up with information on where things stand. Without you following up, they could easily assume you did nothing. Your commitment to follow up will also help you remain accountable for providing an update, even if the news isn't what was hoped for. It takes courage to be transparent and honest, and it's that kind of courage that builds trust and deepens relationships.

Set Aside Your Emotions to Be Fully Present for Others

The decision to create an open forum can be unnerving at times. It may be tempting to gloss over challenging topics when you're not sure what may come up. People may have feedback that is hard to hear. The feedback may even be directed at you. Rather than glossing over issues, your willingness to sit with the discomfort of what is said and the way you model it for others reinforces trust within the team. More than that, your discussion may be instrumental to bringing a solution to fruition. This result, though, hinges on your ability to keep your emotions in check. Find your neutral and stay there as you listen to the feedback, especially when you've invited it.

I've witnessed leaders asking employees questions where they sought gratitude or exaltation for the privilege of working for them or in their company. Sometimes it turned out that way, sometimes it didn't. It's a reminder, though, that in order to be present and provide safety for others, you need to keep your own emotions and insecurities in check. Deepening understanding means being OK with feedback that may be difficult or uncomfortable. Navigating through moments of tension, disappointment, and conflict is the reason for the conversation—so you can arrive on the other side.

Even at home this happens. More times than I want to admit, I have elicited responses from my children to make me feel better rather than inviting honest conversation about how they are feeling. I recall my daughter coming home from her first day in middle school. She walked in the door, and I eagerly greeted her and enthusiastically congratulated her on this momentous day. While she set down her backpack, my mother called, and I immediately thrust the phone at my daughter so she could tell Grandma how cool it was to be in middle school. My daughter pleasantly carried on a brief conversation with her grandmother. After hanging up the phone, she turned down a snack and went to her room. I went in to talk with her, and she immediately broke into tears. She described how two of her best friends had bullied her with texts and refused to talk to her. I was devastated. And then angry at her friends. And then ashamed at how I had made my need to feel that everything was great more important than being present with my daughter when she literally needed a shoulder to cry on. Had I been more empathetic, I would have noticed that my daughter had started a conversation when she walked in the door, not by what she said, but by how she had seemed.

Let's Take a Pause

There are some conversations you enter into that may feel as though they've already begun. You see that someone is angry, and you make assumptions as to why; they didn't like the joke you made at the outset of the meeting, they just got some upsetting news about staff reductions, or perhaps someone dinged their car in the parking lot. Whatever it is, they are now in your line of sight, and you have things to run by them. Seeing that they are upset, perhaps even angry with you for some reason, you are confronted with a decision: Is this a time to walk away or try to understand? Your choice will depend on how well you know this person and how critical it is that you get their input now.

In a heightened emotional state, people have more difficulty responding to questions. If they are trying to hold it together emotionally, asking them questions may cause them to shut down and may even add to their frustration. Consider starting with an observation instead of a question.

- *You seem really upset.*
- *I sense your frustration.*
- *What a busy week!*
- *I heard you're short-staffed.*
- *We're all confused now.*
- *This isn't going smoothly.*

These kinds of statements acknowledge the situation without requiring an explanation. Even if you're in a hurry, this simple step may take only a few minutes. As an added bonus, it may pave the way to getting the input you need, while also nurturing your relationship with this person and conveying your willingness to listen. Validating what's going on or how someone may be feeling will often help people to let down their guard and relax. They will open up when they are ready.

Preparing Others for Your Feedback

Paradoxically, when planning to give difficult feedback to someone, **start** with preparing yourself. Ask yourself, "What am I feeling right now?" If you are outraged, beyond coping with a situation, ready to "let them have it," or you can't believe you are having to tell them the same thing *yet again*, then wait. Unless the person is in physical danger and you need to take action to keep them safe, just wait. Do not provide feedback when you are angry or frustrated. Wait until you calm down; take time to plan what you want to say. You may want to write down a few talking points to help you stay on point. Doing these things will help keep the focus on the other person's performance or behavior as opposed to making it about yours.

As hard as it may be to **start** a conversation, recognize that for the person you are talking with, it may be painful or alarming to receive feedback they weren't expecting. Recognizing this helps to strategize ways to move into a conversation. If you anticipate defensiveness, for example, you may want to have some requests ready to help move things forward.

- *We need to talk.*
- *We see things differently.*
- *Let's get this sorted.*
- *Let's assume positive intent.*
- *Please hear me out.*
- *You'll get equal time.*
- *Please don't interrupt me.*
- *I won't interrupt you.*

By taking a few minutes to explain what you are seeking and what your expectations are for how the conversation will go, you'll give the other person time to prepare. You don't start every conversation this way. When you are meeting and greeting, when the stakes are low, you can easily dive into talking with each other. It's when the **stakes are high** or the content of the conversation is challenging—for both the person initiating and the person on the receiving end—that setting the tone for the conversation can help navigate the way forward. Just remember to slow it down, be still, and allow the other person to respond and **ask questions**. Focus on mutually deepening understanding and connection to improve or resolve situations that come up.

Try This

Think about some of the most common questions or greetings that come up in conversations. As quickly as you can, on your own or with a partner, write down as many questions as you can and come up with where the most predictable response would be "Fine," "No," "OK," or "Yes?" *You might even make it a game*. Set your timer for sixty seconds and challenge yourself or others to come up with examples as fast as you can. Here are a few to get you started:

- *How was your weekend?*
- *How did it go?*
- *How are you today?*
- *How was your day?*
- *How are you feeling?*
- *How was the show?*

On your own, over the next few days, notice how commonly these questions come up in conversations intended to build connection. Consider how you could reword these questions in ways that would invite more interaction and discussion. For instance, instead of "How was the show?" you might ask, "What part of the show did you like best?" Or "What's something fun you did last weekend?" instead of "How was your weekend?" If doing this with a partner, compare notes about what you've observed and tried.

Reflect

In the spirit of inclusivity and understanding, who are the people you naturally gravitate toward and invite into conversation? What do those people have in common with you? Consider who you aren't naturally inclined to connect with; why or why not? What are some ways that you could build more connections with people who you are less familiar with? What are some potential benefits to deepening your connections with these people?

Four More Words to Deepen Understanding and Connection

- *We're different; it's OK.*
- *We hear things differently.*
- *What are you hearing?*
- *I'm challenged by this.*
- *What do you think?*
- *Your perspective is important.*
- *Thanks for trusting me.*
- *My door remains open.*

Four More Words

Jot down some of your four-word phrases **to deepen understanding and connection.**

My Four Words

My Four Words

ten

what not to say

Four Words at a Glance

- *Over my dead body.*
- *You're wrong about that.*
- *Here we go again.*
- *I already told you.*
- *I demand an apology.*
- *Let's see who wins.*
- *I'm going to HR.*
- *I was just kidding.*
- *It's you, not me.*
- *Good luck with that.*
- *You are overly sensitive.*
- *Who made you queen?*

Allow me to save you the trouble of trying out any of these. There are some expressions that, four words or not, are just not going to land well. I realize that for some of you reading this, you will take my advice as a challenge. Gauntlet thrown down, you may be determined to try them anyway. But trust me. I've been doing this a long time, and I rarely see any of these expressions work well unless shared—as will be the case here—for illustrative purposes, or in extremely rare cases, for fun.

It's true that in certain settings, even the most abrupt or outrageous responses may prove funny. Comedians entertain us by intentionally saying things we wouldn't dare say or get away with in real life. Comedian Mike Birbiglia points out in his Netflix comedy special, *Thank God for Jokes*, that for any joke to be funny, someone has to be offended. Point taken, Mr. Birbiglia. And note that while he gets paid for being offensive, other folks risk being fired.

Anyone Can Be Triggered

Triggering phrases evoke heightened emotional responses, ones that are often negative or defensive. Some derogatory words and phrases are predictably triggering and widely understood to be inappropriate. Others are more subtle. For example, notice how a perfectly fine name like Karen became slang for something entirely different. When I grew up, "postal" meant we were mailing something. Now, referring to "postal" signals the potential for violence.

Even the word "triggering" could be triggering to some. Personally, I bristle when people refer to being "shot down" or "caught in the crosshairs." These phrases hit close to home not only because of the growing incidents of gun violence and mass shootings, but my son, then working in retail, had been held up at gunpoint multiple times during a night of rioting in 2020. It's things like this that remind us that we never fully know people's hot buttons. More often, we tend to bump into them by saying something that causes an unintended response.

To avoid these issues, the widely accepted advice is "know your audience." While you may have a general sense, be prepared to be surprised. Kristina, another colleague of mine, shared an experience she had when delivering training to women at a shelter for victims of domestic abuse. As Kristina instructed the women in ways to handle difficult situations, she commented on a "rule of thumb." As soon as the words left her mouth, the vibe in the group shifted; a few of the women became angry. Kristina asked what was wrong. "Have I offended you?" she asked. The answer was a resounding "Yes!"

The women explained that "rule of thumb" was a historical legal reference indicating the acceptable diameter of a stick that men could use to beat their wives; hitting a wife with a stick bigger in diameter than the thickness of one's thumb was against the law. Neither Kristina nor I had ever heard that before. More importantly, at the time of the training, Kristina did not debate the point, nor did she feel compelled to Google the point to see if what they told her was accurate. Upon learning that she had offended her audience, Kristina apologized, thanked the women for their insight, and made a single, slight adjustment by referring to "general rule" instead.

In my own experience facilitating workshops all over the country for different industries, even after doing my homework to understand the perspectives and sensitivities of people I will be speaking to, I have no way of knowing how things will land for each person individually. Like Kristina, I can't guard against every case, and neither can you. That's why a few thoughtful decisions made ahead of time about phrases to avoid is beneficial. Unless you are Eddie Murphy, it's probably best not to use phrases, especially at work, that you anticipate people having a negative reaction to.

Other Hot Buttons May Be Subtle or Hard to Predict

Beyond phrases that may be predictably offensive or divisive, there are other phrases that may be more specific to an individual that they find sufficiently annoying, causing them to become irritated or upset. For instance, my husband becomes annoyed when he asks me something, and I tell him that I'd told him already. Our conversational dance used to go something like this:

Me: "I told you already."

Him: "No, you didn't."

Me: "Yes, I'm confident I did."

Him: "No, I'm pretty sure you didn't."

When we were first married, I would sometimes make it worse by describing in detail where we were standing, what I was wearing, what we were eating, and who else was there. Hoping he'd recall events as I had, I also sometimes tried to prove I was right. (We're both lawyers incidentally.) It didn't work. Worse, beyond aggravating a simple misunderstanding, it introduced an unnecessary and disruptive rift in our relationship, resulting in temporary hurt and distrust. Happily married for over thirty years, I don't do this anymore. Knowing his hot buttons, I happily avoid them. Who wins in this instance? Both of us.

This example highlights that what one person remembers versus how another recalls an experience is one of those disagreements that generally cannot be solved. Without a transcript or video of what was said or not said, everyone is left to their respective points of view. Arguing the point only deepens the tension without serving our relationship or clarifying the intended information. It also confuses the issue. This argument is not so much about what was or wasn't said. Underneath all of this he said/she said drama is sensitivity to the suggestion that one's memory is failing or that one is more attentive than the other.

Discovering individuals' hot buttons is a process. Incident by incident, hot buttons are revealed as people take offense to what you've unwittingly said or done. These instances show up without warning, but once revealed, you can add them to your list of "phrases to avoid."

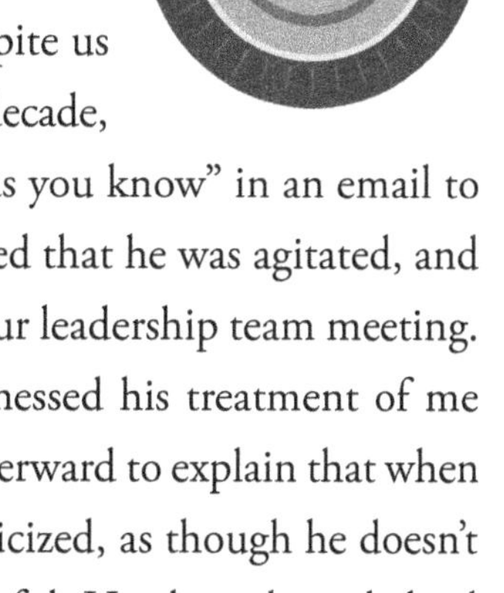

One phrase I learned to avoid with a senior leader I knew well is "as you know." Despite us having worked closely together for over a decade, I learned this the hard way after I used "as you know" in an email to him. My next encounter with him revealed that he was agitated, and I was getting the brunt of his ire during our leadership team meeting. With prompting from others who'd witnessed his treatment of me during the meeting, he approached me afterward to explain that when someone says "as you know," he feels criticized, as though he doesn't know something he should or he is forgetful. He also acknowledged that there was no way that I could have known this, and he was sorry for the way he had reacted. With this newfound knowledge, I added "as you know" and "like I just said" to the list of phrases I would avoid using with him and others.

Your Personal Hot Buttons

When your own hot buttons are pushed, you can choose to be defensive or you can take the high road. The high road means that you avoid aggravating a situation. That may mean allowing the other person to talk while you give space. It may also mean that rather than responding in the moment, you can briefly acknowledge the other person's comment, and then you take a pause.

- *Give me some time.*
- *I'm thinking about this.*
- *I'm surprised by this.*
- *Let me come back.*

You may even suggest that when you reconnect for the conversation, you both bring specific examples or potential solutions. Maintaining focus on the desired outcome whether it be a change in behavior or a problem to be solved, will help to instill collaboration and understanding. Look for the win-win option as opposed to the "drop the mic" moment. Your relationship and perhaps even your career will be better for it.

Be Prepared to Intervene

Great work rarely results when people are at odds with each other. When you hear people blaming and threatening each other, respond as though it were your personal call to action. In the heat of the moment, things said or left unaddressed may be long remembered and destroy trust. Even when leaders haven't said anything offensive, their failure to address problems may cause them to lose **credibility**.

At work, professionalism rules the day. It's not enough to monitor your own statements, and especially if you are in leadership, be mindful of what you model for others and be prepared to intervene or redirect. Be prepared to step in to prevent things from escalating when you hear statements like these directed at you or someone on your team:

- *You never truly listen.*
- *You're such a jerk.*
- *You better watch out.*
- *You could be next.*

- *You're always picking fights.*
- *You figure it out.*

These kinds of statements come from people who are overwhelmed and just plain over it. We hear anger, frustration, and defensiveness. More than shutting down a conversation, divisive and dismissive statements are symptomatic of unresolved underlying issues. Take stock of the bigger picture—and take action. Impulsive responses like these may have dire consequences, inciting additional escalation. Retaliatory remarks may also put careers and relationships at risk—especially if it happens more than once.

Repairing Relationships and Reputation

Popular memes and celebrity tweets may be provocative but rarely play well in professional or work settings. In short, what the Kardashians may get away with is not instructive for what works well for others. Worse, as is perennially demonstrated in news headlines, entire careers may be jeopardized by stray comments. For most of us, though, what's at stake in the more immediate sense is the trust and rapport you work to establish at work and at home. Even when no harm is intended, your relationships and **credibility** may be on the line.

Part of my coaching practice involves working with high-profile individuals who have engaged in inappropriate behavior. My friend Bruce describes me as "the Fixer." I once worked with a member of a professional sports team, who I'll refer to as Chris. Chris was observed by fans making inappropriate jokes and comments in a public venue. Before meeting with him, I had viewed footage of the incident that someone had recorded on their phone and posted on YouTube. I'd also seen the press conference where the lawyer for offended fans replayed the event. I knew a lot about what happened before I met with this individual, but I hadn't heard his side of the story.

We spoke about what happened; he described being with his teammates and they were joking with each other and not cognizant of anyone else being around. He was mortified later when he learned that someone had recorded their conversation. He was also remorseful—not for having been caught, but for offending fans and bringing negative publicity to his team. Chris was accountable for his actions and accepted the consequences. Independent of the disciplinary measures, Chris still had the task of restoring his **credibility** and his relationships with the team. We talked about how to do this. Again, it comes down to a few words.

- *I accept my responsibility.*
- *I regret my actions.*
- *I understand the consequences.*
- *I've learned from this.*
- *This won't happen again.*

Not everyone gets a second chance, but in this instance, Chris did. When I met with him a month after our initial meeting, he told me what it was like to return to work after his suspension. He confessed being anxious about what kind of reception he might expect from his peers when he entered the locker room. Where he thought they might be dismissive or resentful, they surprised him by welcoming him back. Gathering around Chris, one team member, speaking on behalf of the rest of the team, said, "We're glad you're back. This is for you." They handed him an envelope filled with cash. "This should cover your salary for the time that you were suspended. We all pitched in, because we feel like we owe it to you. You took one for the team.

What happened to you could have happened to any of us, and this was a valuable lesson for us all. We need to be better."

- *We are a team.*
- *We can do better.*
- *We are learning together.*
- *Let's raise the bar.*
- *We model our values.*
- *We coach each other.*

Being Accountable

Being human, we will all make mistakes from time to time; there will be misunderstandings; we'll cause unintended harm. Accepting that this is true without making others wrong for their interpretations of our actions isn't always easy, but it does get easier with practice. In one-to-one situations at work or at home, acknowledging responsibility for the hurt regardless whether it was intended is paramount. There is nuance in this, however. You may intend to apologize for something by saying, "I'm sorry you're hurting" or "I'm sorry you feel that way." The person on the other side of this may understand that you regret how they interpreted your actions, instead of you being accountable for what you did. Similarly, "I'm sorry you took it that way," sounds more like a criticism for how the person took it than an apology for something you said or did.

Instead, focus on your behavior—what you did or didn't do. Be specific; you need not constrain your comments to four words here. Clearly communicate that you understand the concerns and how you may have contributed to the issue. To either of the following, briefly explain your actions or behavior and avoid talking, at least initially, about your feelings or intentions.

- *I'm sorry I said that.*
- *You're right, I shouldn't haven't done that.*
- *Is there anything else you'd like me to know?*

It's not easy to ask if there is anything else when you are already regretting what you said or did initially. By asking, you are also conveying that you are willing to hear what others have to say. It can be hard to be silent and listen. You may feel unfairly criticized or misunderstood. Arguing your intentions or suggesting how the other person should feel instead are not likely to repair the relationship.

How the other person feels or reacts is their own business. You can't control how they will take something you said or did. There is no value in arguing right and wrong, reasonable or unreasonable. Let it go.

Focus on your actions and keep the goal of reconciliation at the forefront. No blaming, no shaming, no vilifying. If the relationship matters, then wholeheartedly work to repair it.

- *That must've been hard.*
- *I understand this now.*
- *I'd be lonely too.*
- *Thanks for your honesty.*
- *I understand your perspective.*
- *I care about your feelings.*
- *I value our friendship.*
- *Let's work this out.*

Fail forward, as a colleague of mine advocates. Lean into rebuilding the break in fellowship. More often than not, what comes out of these moments of reconciliation is a strong bond and deeper trust.

The Gift of Feedback

When coaching leaders struggle to respond to feedback they don't like and may even disagree with, I ask them to imagine that the information they receive is a gift. It may not be something they were seeking but imagining the feedback as arriving at their door in a Tiffany-blue box with a bow on it. This briefly refocuses attention on the giver and what their intention was in providing the feedback. Rarely do people say things at work with the intention to be mean, though the way the information is delivered may come out that way. Looking for the truth or insight in the feedback helps to slow down a response that may aggravate an already-tense situation. For example, an employee may be critical of her boss for always taking credit for her ideas. The boss, hearing the accusation, may immediately respond with, "I don't do that!" Each of them may have examples, each may dig in more, and each of them will trust each other less than before, unless the leader responds differently and considers what positive intent the employee may have in bringing this up. Is the employee just mad, or is it possible she's asking to be seen and heard in a way that the leader inadvertently has overlooked? The leader, instead of rejecting a perceived accusation, might instead see this exchange as a gift, inviting the two of them to come to a better understanding of what each other needs and how they might work together better.

- *Would you give examples?*
- *I didn't intend that.*
- *You deserve the credit.*
- *Your contributions are substantial.*
- *I'll let others know.*
- *Thanks for telling me.*

Listening intently doesn't require that you agree. We can't learn, though, if we don't listen. Receive the feedback, and then you can decide what you want to do with it. Just don't take it out on the person bearing what you perceive to be bad news. The feedback you receive may hold great value to you in your career … if you accept it as a gift.

Try This

With a partner or in a small group, come up with short phrases you believe wouldn't be likely to go well as a conversation starter or a response to someone who is initiating a conversation. Write these phrases down on Post-it notes or index cards and collect them in a bowl. Invite people to share a recent example in which they spoke with a family member, neighbor, or coworker about something that was bothering them. Keep it light. Here are some examples:

- My neighbor "accidentally" opened my delivery from Amazon and apparently went through the contents before bringing it over.
- My coworker asked me to come into the office early to help her with a project, and she didn't show up.
- It's nine at night, and my daughter just told me she needs to bring two dozen cupcakes to school tomorrow morning.
- My boss insists he told me about the deadline, but I'm positive he never mentioned it.

Now randomly pull out and read aloud one of the responses from the bowl. Discuss how that response might go and brainstorm other alternatives that might smooth the situation and maintain the relationship.

Reflect

You can choose to be right, clever, respected, or trusted. You can choose to respond in ways that deepen connection or weaken it. Whichever you choose, do you like your reasons? Do you like your results? Is there a recent example where you would want to show up differently than you did? What would you do differently?

Four More Words

Jot down any four-word phrases **you want to avoid using.**

Over my dead body!

Good luck with that!

eleven

when it's not working

Four Words at a Glance

- *I'd like to explain.*
- *Let's quit walking away.*
- *We can do this.*
- *It's not rocket science.*

My friend Mike, a Fulbright scholar with a doctorate in philosophy, was immediately skeptical when I explained that I was writing a book on how to start conversations with as few as four thoughtfully chosen words. I wasn't surprised. I know we live in a complex, dynamic, turbulent world, and the issues facing us are too crucial to be reduced to four-word phrases.

My goal, though, in writing this book, is not to solve the world's problems. Instead, let's focus on your challenges. In particular, I want to encourage you to have conversations you have been avoiding. If the tips in this book ultimately support an end to homelessness and hunger, promote world peace or a better world for generations to come, that's a bonus. After I explained this to Mike, he relented a bit.

"I guess that might work," he said. "As long as you don't fetishize the number four."

"Four Words" Is a Call to Action, Not a Rule

In all honesty, as I look back on many of the examples I share in this book, there are plenty of instances where a phrase of five, six, or even eight words, may be more eloquent or sound more familiar. But I repeatedly see in my own conversations and those I observe that fewer words often maximizes both **clarity** and impact. Expressing points of view or asking for clarification without preamble or apology conveys more confidence. Paring back what you have to say and omitting things like, "This may be a silly question, but …" or "I'm sorry for saying this but …" and getting to the point helps maintain focus on the issues at hand.

- *I have an idea.*
- *This is not working.*
- *I vote Option C.*
- *This isn't adding up.*
- *Who authorized this expense?*

Keep it **simple**. Choose your words, however many it turns out to be, with **brevity** in mind.

And don't apologize for respectfully offering your opinion. By sharing your opinion, speaking up, asking for what you want, healing misunderstandings, and strengthening collaboration, you open yourself up to new possibilities for fulfillment and advancement. As a leader, this is particularly true. The people around you deserve to know what's on your mind. Let folks know what you need from them and **ask questions** to better understand what they need from you.

I'm not guaranteeing that four words works for everyone or in every situation.

So, what do you do when four-word phrases aren't working for you? Some of you may choose to give up and go back to avoiding conversations. Others may want to proclaim this whole concept as absurd. Still others may actively seek out ways to demonstrate how this concept simply won't work. But if you're overly rigid about *four words, and only four words,* you may be missing the point. I'm suggesting that by succinctly starting a conversation, you may achieve more results than if you ruminate over talking to someone, or altogether avoid the exchange.

- *It's not for everything.*
- *It's not for everyone.*
- *More than four words is OK.*
- *You can also abort mission if it's not working.*

Once Started, Keep Going

Four words are enough to spark a conversation. Four words can also be used as a tool to focus responses. And four words can reengage conversation when there is a breakdown. It's the adaptive quality of this simple strategy that does more than "grease the skids" for initiating interaction.

- *Where are we at?*
- *What have we decided?*
- *Where are we stuck?*
- *Who's responsible for what?*
- *What is the timeline?*
- *What's our next step?*
- *What is our plan?*

These questions bring attention to the issues at hand and keep the conversation moving forward. They are time-tested in coaching, mediation, production, scheduling, and project management. I think they would have worked well, too, with our kids when they were teens, but I hadn't figured that out yet. If you try any of these techniques with your kids, I'd love to hear about it!

A Note of Caution

There are instances when conversations should be avoided or aborted. In this age of so much gun violence and growing numbers of persons with mental illness, your safety is paramount. *Let's be careful out there.* Be smart. Some conversations are better left to the experts. Understand your surroundings and avoid putting yourself in harm's way.

When I was practicing law, I had a meeting with a client who I knew had been very angry about having been sued. Though I had not met him yet, I had some preliminary information about his demeanor when he had been interviewed by others, and I was wary about meeting with him. It was not uncommon to meet with clients at a mutually convenient location. In this instance, I knew I wanted backup. I asked him to meet with me at my office. Before he arrived, I also arranged for my secretary to keep the door ajar and "interrupt" us a couple of times during the meeting. In the end, all went well, but I don't regret taking precautions.

Another time, I was supporting a human resources team during a layoff of several shipyard employees. When previous layoffs had occurred, there were some heated interactions between the managers and employees. While no one was hurt, we were more attune to the risk of violence, and we opted to have off-duty police officers on hand for added security and safety.

If you are involved in a conversation, and it is getting heated or breaking down, you have full permission to remove yourself from the situation. But if it's a conversation worth having, don't give up. Consider what resources are available to you to move forward. If it's a conversation at work, your leaders, Human Resources, or other resources may be able to help. Speak up. Your safety is paramount.

Try This

Notice when you tried using a four-word phrase, and you didn't think it worked well. Keep notes of what you tried and consider some alternatives you might have chosen instead. Are there some other five- to eight-word sentences or phrases that you want to add to your "toolbox" to keep the conversation going? Share your observations with others by explaining the scenario and asking them what they think would work best from what you've come up with.

Reflect

Start listening to other people's comments during meetings. What are the phrases they use that detract from a clear statement of their point of view? Do they state their disagreement, or do they qualify what their perspective is? For instance, are you hearing people say, "Some people might not like this, but …" instead of saying what they themselves don't like or agree with? Are people starting a comment by apologizing for it? Do they sometimes say, "This might be a dumb question, but …" or "I may have missed this, but …"?

Think of ways they could have expressed themselves more effectively. Start to notice whether you use preambles and, if so, decide whether you want to do something differently.

Four More Words

"Write down four word phrases to use **when it's not working**, such as:

- *I'm not walking away.*
- *I'm willing to try.*
- *Not everything is perfect.*

My Four Words

My Four Words

twelve

what's next?

Words at a Glance

- *Why didn't you tell me?*
- *How could I have known?*
- *How long ago was it?*
- *Where do we go now?*
- *Let's keep experimenting with this.*
- *I think we're getting somewhere.*

As I was writing this book, I kept joking with friends that the next book would be called *The Next Five Words*. No doubt as you've been reading and coming up with your own examples, there are many instances where you may have felt that adding another word or two would work better. While I maintain that four words is a good place to start, I've acknowledged along the way that this use of creativity is intended as a way to motivate you to **start** the conversation, and it is not intended to be a rigid rule. At the end of the day, it doesn't really matter how few words you use to start or continue a conversation. My goal is quite simply to **inspire** you to get beyond your reasons for not initiating conversations and show up with greater ease and confidence.

The art is in the start.

Whether it's the first four words, the next five words, or any other approach that works for you, the measure of success is whether you are making yourself heard and understood. The art is in the **start**.

Starting Is Just the Beginning

In previous chapters, we explored building trust, resolving conflicts, and coming to a consensus. None of these conversations are intended to be reduced to four-word phrases that you lob back and forth to each other. There will be stories and examples to explore. Different points of view will need to be heard and considered; questions asked; clarification sought. Deeper meaning and discovery happens only when the door is opened, *after* the conversation starts.

People sometimes worry that without a script or a model they won't know where to go next. Conversations can be planned, but ultimately they are improvisational. It's like being part of a dance and responding to the next steps.

The good news is that you can use the same strategy to expand the conversation that you used to get it started. There are many four-word phrases available that will help you to continue and conclude conversations. The magic of this simple approach is that by having a few short phrases at the ready, you can be more fully present as the conversation unfolds. With less thinking about what you will say and knowing already some questions to ask or some brief comments to add, you can listen and absorb. You'll also stand a better chance of being heard when you continue your commitment to being succinct.

Adapting and expanding the ways that you employ this four-word strategy can be liberating.

Adding to Your Conversational Toolbox

Here are some **simple** four-word questions to use in a conversation. These questions invite response and demonstrate that you are actively listening and looking to understand other perspectives.

- *How did it feel?*
- *What was your experience?*
- *Was there anything new?*
- *What really surprised you?*
- *What did you learn?*
- *Anything you'd do differently?*
- *What were the takeaways?*

These questions bring to mind many conversations I've had with clients and colleagues. The opportunity for insight and new perspectives are substantial when we create these moments to learn from each other. We also convey, by asking thoughtful questions, that we care and respect each other's points of view. And leaders, this is an ideal way for you to model the types of questions you want team members to be asking of each other and the clients you work with.

Four words are sufficient, too, for closing a conversation. They help to draw the conclusion to a close while ensuring everyone is aligned. For ongoing conversations, take time to schedule or confirm when you will meet again. You may want to go over who will be responsible for what in the interim, before meeting the next time. And here's some easy phrases to use in winding things up.

- *Thank you for listening.*
- *I learned a lot.*
- *Let's review our agreements.*
- *This was really helpful.*
- *Let's meet up again.*
- *Thanks for your time.*
- *See you next week!*

You may be ending the meeting, but you don't want to end the conversation. Your optimism for when you come together again helps to maintain morale and engagement. And it costs nothing.

Rethinking the Conversations You Have in Your Head

Let me invite you into an entirely different conversation that we haven't discussed this far. I'm referring to the conversations you are constantly having with yourself. You know that loop that runs continually in your own head? I may be meddling, but while your internal dialogue is your personal business, everyone has some form of banter inside their own mind. The question I have for you is whether you like what's rumbling around in your head and whether you like your results.

This is an area I spend a lot of time working on with my clients. Unpacking, evaluating, and ultimately deciding whether to accept it or try to shift perspectives and beliefs. You can do this on your own or with a trusted colleague or friend. By asking a few simple questions of yourself, you can start to learn how to interrupt the constant chatter in your brain. Awareness is the first step and comes from asking yourself questions that give pause and invite reflection. You may ask:

- *Do I believe that?*
- *Is it really true?*
- *How do I know?*
- *What if everything's fine?*
- *What if nothing's wrong?*
- *Whose fault is it?*
- *Is that really true?*
- *What could I do?*
- *What would it take?*
- *Could I let go?*
- *How might I start?*
- *Who could help me?*

The power of these simple questions is their ability to illuminate old habits and determine where you've been on autopilot. These are the kinds of questions that I ask clients seeking to make changes. As the saying goes, if you want better answers, it invariably starts with asking better questions. While it's not four words, one of my favorite questions to ask my clients is, "*How do you actually know what you think you know?*" Often they discover that what they think they know is based on a narrative they've constructed, not fact. When we ask ourselves these kinds of questions, interrogating what we've understood to be reality, we find that it's just a story—and stories can be rewritten. They also often turn out better than we imagine.

Women Leaders Take Note

While this book is for all leaders and aspiring leaders, I would be remiss if I did not point out that women leaders often benefit from additional support to overcome ways they are socially predisposed to prioritizing the needs of others over their own. You most likely know this as people pleasing, playing nice, and avoiding conflict. There are numerous and complex reasons why this is. Rather than focusing on root causes, I've offered some simple strategies and examples to overcome the tendency to shy away from opinions and hard conversations. Your voice matters, and everyone stands to gain from diverse perspectives.[30]

Studies demonstrate that women experience more self-doubt as compared to their male counterparts.[31] Expected to be competent but not assertive, women are often uncertain about how to present themselves at work. Learning to speak up for yourself not only expands your confidence, but also it may help you save your sanity and your health, if not your very life. In *The Myth of Normal*, Dr. Gabor Maté explains suppressing anger and self-silencing leads to high blood pressure—making them potential silent killers. Convincing yourself to play it safe by keeping your opinions quiet may be detrimental to you and those around you.

While it's not always easy to be **brave**, the positive benefits may surprise you. In a 2016 Story Corp interview, Ashley Judd shared that after being afraid to come forward with her accusations about Harvey Weinstein's sexual harassment of her, she realized that her

---

30 FearlessBR, "Leading Fearlessly: Why Women Improve Results in the Boardroom but Still Need a Seat at the Table," FearlessBR, March 8, 2022, https://fearlessbr.com/leading-fearlessly-women-improve-results-in-the-boardroom-but-still-need-a-seat-at-the-table/.;

Jenny M. Hoobler, Grace Lemmon, and Stella M. Nkomo, "Research: Adding Women to the C-Suite Changes How Companies Think," *Harvard Business Review*, April 12, 2021, https://hbr.org/2021/04/research-adding-women-to-the-c-suite-changes-how-companies-think.;

Tomas Chamorro Premuzic, "The Business Case for Women in Leadership," *Forbes*, March 2, 2022, https://www.forbes.com/sites/tomaspremuzic/2022/03/02/the-business-case-for-women-in-leadership/.; McKinsey & Company, "Women in the Workplace," McKinsey.com, accessed February 9, 2024, https://www.mckinsey.com/featured-insights/diversity-and-inclusion/women-in-the-workplace.

31 Jack Zenger, "The Confidence Gap in Men and Women: Why It Matters and How to Overcome It," *Forbes*, April 8, 2018, https://www.forbes.com/sites/jackzenger/2018/04/08/the-confidence-gap-in-men-and-women-why-it-matters-and-how-to-overcome-it/.

silence was costing her too much. Deciding to come forward, she said, was scary; she described it as feeling like she had flung "the barn doors wide open," and the horses had run out. A stampede like that might prove terrifying, but once set in motion, she reflected, "The joy of the stampede surprised me. I didn't know it would be so joyous."

Ladies, that's what I want for you—to experience the joy of bravely and confidently speaking up, no matter what the topic. I also want you to know that it can be a whole lot simpler than you imagine.

Campfire Connection

At some of my workshops, I show a picture of people gathered around an evening campfire. I bring the lights down, and I invite people to imagine that they, too, are sitting around the campfire. This is a place of warmth, gathering, stories, and laughter. This is the place where the events of the day are talked about, plans are made for tomorrow, and people put their arms around each other while sharing memories and s'mores.

I had a teacher who frequently reminded his students that the best moments in life are the corny, mushy ones. It's the simple joys of being alive and surrounded by those you love that sustain us. These times are also made possible by our commitment to maintaining honesty with each other and showing genuine care and affection.

At work, these times are rare and often show up in the in-between times, before or after the business part of the day. They may happen over a shared meal, a business trip, in the ten minutes or so at the end of a video call when everyone else has signed off and there are just two or three employees remaining on the line. Sometimes they occur while walking out to the parking lot together at the end of the day, where employees exchange their plans for the evening or reflect on the day's work. Unscripted and unplanned, these are the campfire moments that deserve to be acknowledged.

- *Hey, that went well!*
- *I like working together.*
- *This has been fun.*
- *I appreciate your help.*
- *Thanks for the ideas.*

What you say in these moments doesn't have to be a big deal. There is no need for production in these times. Rather, a few words in these shared moments in which you convey appreciation or celebrate a win are part of what connects you to each other and reinforces collaboration. Start looking for these moments and acting on them. Remember, people will always remember how you made them feel more than anything else.

Try This

Jot down the names of everyone that you regularly interact with. For each of these people, write down two or three things that you appreciate or admire about them.

Sometimes this is difficult when there is tension or hard feelings with people you work with. If you are having a hard time coming up with something, imagine what their life partner or their child would say about them. Stepping outside of workday roles and responsibilities and looking to see people through the perspective of someone that loves them may help you appreciate qualities and connections that you can begin looking for in the context of your work together. When I've applied this technique in the past, I discovered connections and shared hobbies with others, such as a love of dogs, action figure toys for our kids, and travel. These shared interests, once discovered, were somewhat of a secret alliance that we had formed, unrelated to the current project or meeting agenda.

Reflect

Who are the people who have been instrumental to you at work and in life? Try to name at least five of the most important ones. If it were possible and you had nothing to lose, **what would you tell each of them about the impact they've had on your life?**

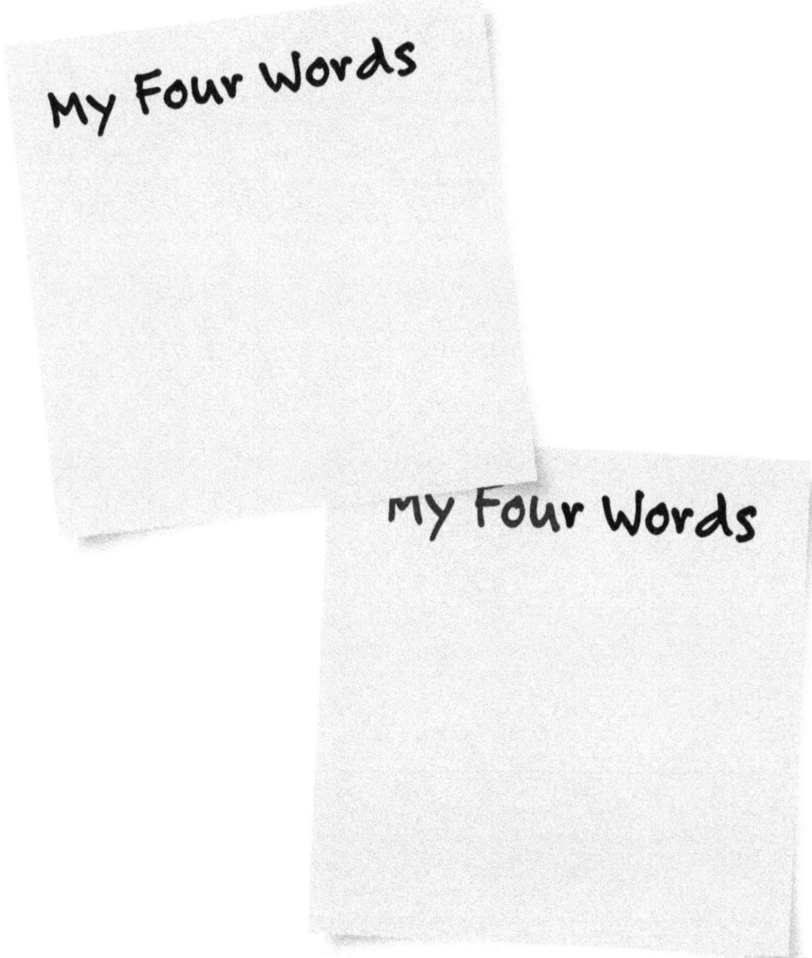

conclusion

Words at a Glance

- *I just finished this.*
- *Have you read it?*
- *Let's experiment with it.*
- *This is so simple!*
- *I'm ready for anything.*

It's much easier than you think, when it comes to overcoming the inclination to avoid talking with people at work, a networking event, or a family gathering. In as few as four words, an entire dynamic can shift. The biggest shift, though, is often the one that happens in our own minds. When we move beyond fear, doubt, and excuses, and start challenging ourselves to think of four words that *might just work to get things started*, we're already halfway there. As when you are solving a puzzle, you start to wonder, what if what you come up with actually works? How will you know if you don't try? Let's do it. Let's find out if your hunch was right. If it doesn't work, what have you lost? More often than

In as few as four words, an entire dynamic can shift.

not, even if you fumble, or if you use more than four words, the conversation will likely still happen.

Your Call to Action

Learning comes from application; knowing is informed by doing. I've given you lots of ideas and exercises throughout this book. Put pen to paper and take some notes. Write in this book. Build your list of phrases you want to test, and keep track of what works. Most of all, I hope you now find yourself more willing to engage in conversations you'd previously shied away from.

And Finally ...

Alas, my final words for you are more than four:

> *Imagine the possibilities that you can create*
> *with just four words.*
> *Believe in yourself.*
> *Show up. Have the conversation.*
> *See what happens.*

If you'd like to tell me about it, I'd be delighted to hear from you. You can connect with me through my website, www.JTucker-Miller.com, or LinkedIn. You may be interested in checking out the companion workbook I've created to accompany this book. I have also prepared a resource list of First Four Words that is available at my website. Please contact me if you'd like more information about the workshops and keynotes to introduce and expand on the ideas I've discussed in this book.

acknowledgments

Thank you to my family. I have loved, learned, practiced, and sometimes failed in conversations with each of you, and I am humbled by the ways that we remain deeply committed to each other. It's been a lot of fun experimenting with the concepts in this book, and I appreciate your humor and support through it all.

A special thanks goes to my husband, Warner, who has contributed to this book through numerous hours of conversation and more. You have always been my person.

Thank you to my clients, friends, and colleagues for the ways you have touched my life. You have been among my greatest supporters, mentors, and collaborators. I've been enriched profoundly by our relationships and our work together. I am better for the lessons and connections we've shared.

Finally, thank you to my publishing team at Authority Advantage and for your enthusiasm for this effort. It has been both richly rewarding and reassuring to learn that I wasn't crazy for thinking this might be an idea worth sharing.

www.ingramcontent.com/pod-product-compliance
Lightning Source LLC
Chambersburg PA
CBHW022126080426
42734CB00006B/252
* 9 7 8 1 6 4 2 2 5 9 7 7 3 *